Are Your Parents Driving You Crazy?

**Award winner in self-help (*Independent Publisher*),
and self-help Book of the Year finalist
(*ForeWord* magazine)**

"How to resolve problems . . . and keep your sanity throughout is the focus of this practical book . . . There is helpful advice, too, on how to assess the difficulty of resolving a problem . . . Wisely, the authors observe that as long as parents are capable of making decisions, they have a right to manage their lives as they see fit [unless] their health and safety are at immediate risk."—**The New York Times**

"I often recommend this remarkable little book to clients. Straightforward, practical, and helpful, it reflects unusually clear thinking and an excellent grasp of the complex problems faced by elderly people and their adult children."—**Roni Lang, LCSW, Director, Geriatric Assessment Program and Family Caregiver Support Program, Stamford Health System, Stamford, CT**

"[This book] will save you immense amounts of stressful anxiety and bewildered frustration—as well as substantially improve the quality and effectiveness of your efforts on behalf of your aging parents."—**The Midwest Book Review**

"Wonderful resource for adult children. It takes the 'overwhelming' out of problem-solving with a concise process. A

'Linus blanket' you can share with clients and friends."—**Sharmon H. French, LCSW, Chancellor, Gardens of Southington Assisted Living Community**

"Straightforward text . . . a problem-solving model that anyone can use with his or her aging parents . . . an excellent choice for parents, adult children, caretakers, and other health professionals."—*Library Journal*

"Those of us in the field of long-term care know where to look for help once ADL [activities of daily living] deficiencies arise. But what do you do in the meantime, when Mom and Dad need some help, but they cling stubbornly to their independence? That puzzle is why this new book caught our eye . . . This book offers a sensible conceptual framework for understanding the problems and discerning solutions. It provides practical advice that sounds relatively easy to follow. One can readily imagine that difficulties like these, thoughtfully and tactfully addressed, could prevent or delay the need for institutional care."—*LTC Bullets,* **online newsletter**

"The book lets you focus on the problem where there is neither 'I am right' or 'you are wrong' in the solution. I would wholeheartedly recommend this book for anyone with aging parents. The fact is that they will always be the parent, and you the child, and you must always respect that—with love and dignity."—**Lee Darrow, *Lebanon (MO) Daily Record***

Getting to Yes with Competent Aging Parents

Are
Your
Parents
Driving
You
Crazy?

SECOND EDITION

JOSEPH A. ILARDO, PhD, LCSW
CAROLE R. ROTHMAN, PhD

VanderWyk & Burnham

To Christina Ilardo, now 96, who has continued to teach us
a thing or two since this book was first published.

Published by VanderWyk & Burnham
P.O. Box 2789, Acton, Massachusetts 01720

This publication is sold with the understanding that the publisher is not engaged in rendering legal, medical, psychiatric, or other professional services. If expert assistance is required, the services of a competent professional person should be sought.

This book is available for quantity purchases. For information on bulk discounts, call (800) 789-7916 or write to Special Sales at the above address.

www.VandB.com

Library of Congress Cataloging-in-Publication Data
Ilardo, Joseph A.
   Are your parents driving you crazy? : getting to yes with competent aging parents / Joseph A. Ilardo, Carole R. Rothman.— 2nd ed.
       p. cm.
   Summary: "Problem-solving model for people whose parents are still competent and living on their own but showing signs of aging--for example, they should stop driving but won't, or they refuse in-home help even though they need it. Includes ways to break impasses, and act in partnership with parents"— Provided by publisher.
   Includes bibliographical references and index.
   ISBN 1-889242-18-7
   1. Aging parents. 2. Parent and adult child. 3. Older people--Family relationships. I. Rothman, Carole R. (Carole Ronnie), 1945- II. Title.
   HQ1063.6.I43 2006
   306.874'084'6--dc22
                                                            2005019804

Interior book design by Bruce Bond.

FIRST PRINTING
Manufactured in the United States of America
10 9 8 7 6 5 4 3 2 1

Contents

Preface

❧

When we wrote the first edition of *Are Your Parents Driving You Crazy?* we did so for an American audience, expecting it to be useful for adult children who were struggling in their attempts to help their competent older parents. However, there were a few surprises in store for us. To our delight, foreign language rights were purchased; the book was published in Germany, Japan, and Poland. We never expected our thoughts and advice would transcend cultures and geographic boundaries.

We were also pleased to discover that frustrated seniors were buying our book, but to our chagrin, unexpected feedback from many of them made us aware that well-meaning children are just as likely to drive their parents crazy as the other way around. Children err primarily by trying to do more for their parents than the parents want or need. As a result of our heightened awareness, we have added a section that will help children avoid making such errors.

The title of this book appeals to adult children who don't know how to be helpful to their parents and are frustrated by their confusion. These are the readers we hope to reach. Some people may think our title is disrespectful, however, and that it implies the parents are to blame for conflicts between them and their children. Nothing could be further from the truth. While adult children may *feel* that their parents are driving them crazy, there are two sides to every issue, and the child's contribution must be considered as well. In this edition, we continue to bring that point home. We urge parents and children to establish a sound, mutually respectful relationship, which we call the *caring partnership*, and show them how to avoid mistakes that can frustrate their efforts.

Since *Are Your Parents Driving You Crazy?* was first published, we've traveled all over the country, speaking to people of all ages and backgrounds. Two themes remain constant. One is that adult children still complain, "My parents are driving me crazy." The other is that when seniors and their children do try to work out conflicts, they are often unable to reach resolution. We are touched by these well-meaning people who cannot get where they want to go. Their distress motivated us to find additional ways to get our message across. Our underlying beliefs, our approach to "getting to yes," can be summarized in a few basic principles.

First, *everyone has a right to his or her opinions and feelings*, whether or not others agree. No one, from toddler to senior, wants to be told that they should feel or act differently. Second, *there are very few emergencies that require immediate action*. Acting out of panic, before considering alternatives, often leads to poor, sometimes downright disastrous, decisions. Third, *it's impossible to satisfy everyone's needs all the time*. Parents and children who strive to maintain an open relationship must each learn to tolerate some guilt and some frustration. Fourth, *when feelings between parents and children become unusually strong, there's more going on than is immediately apparent.* Unearthing the sources of those feelings is essential to avoid getting sabotaged by them.

As always, we enjoy hearing from readers. If you have a question or an experience to share, please write us in care of VanderWyk & Burnham, P.O. Box 2789, Acton, MA 01720 or e-mail us directly at ircassoc@yahoo.com. We can't promise to answer your letter personally (though we may), but we can promise to read what you say and—hopefully—learn from your experience so that our next edition will be even more helpful than this one.

We want to thank the countless people—friends, clients, radio listeners, members of audiences we've addressed, interviewers—whose struggles and successes increased our awareness of the many faces of eldercare. We thank Eileen Trapp, social worker and assisted living professional, for her insightful and helpful critique of the chapter on assisted living. We also want to thank Meredith Rutter, publisher at VanderWyk & Burnham, for giving us a new opportunity to help adult children and their parents get to yes.

Introduction

❧

Many books are available to help adult children deal with elderly parents suffering from dementia or emotional disorders. This book, however, helps adult children work with parents who are rational and competent but who are not being reasonable about some problem that should be easily resolved. These could be parents who won't go to the doctor when it is clearly called for, or parents who skimp unnecessarily on expenses and put their health and well-being in jeopardy.

Such problems plague adult children of aging parents. And while most problems like these *do* have solutions, finding them isn't easy when it's *your* parents, *your* siblings, and *your* spouse who are involved. You want to do the right thing, but often you don't know what it is, and when you do know, you have no clear idea how to proceed. That is why we wrote this book—to give you the insights and tools to resolve the dilemmas you face and to move forward confidently.

In chapter 1 of "The Context" section, you learn why these dilemmas can present such a challenge when you try to find ways to resolve them. In chapter 2 you read about communication strategies that can increase the chances that you and your parents will resolve the dilemmas together. If you reach a stalemate, chapter 3 can show you how to break the impasse. Then in the last Context chapter, you learn how to keep your sanity through-out the process—by using strategies summarized in the acronym S.U.R.V.I.V.E.

"The Model" section outlines a problem-solving method that will help you resolve any dilemma you are likely to encounter. Our approach is the product of many years of work with adult children such as yourself, and it will serve you well.

In "The Dilemmas" section, you can see how the model works by choosing among twenty-five of the most common dilemmas adult children struggle with. Most of these dilemmas are caused primarily by elderly parents, but some are caused primarily by other members of the family.

As you read through the dilemmas, try not to be too literal. For example, if we describe a situation involving your father, the principles can be applied to your mother or aunt as well. Even if your exact situation doesn't appear here, chances are you will find one or several dilemmas similar enough to be helpful to you. Using the index, you can search for topics related to your own situation that may appear in different dilemmas.

Keep in mind, too, that not all dilemmas will be equally difficult to resolve. Here are some factors that will determine this:

- How many people are involved? (In general, the fewer the people involved, the easier it will be to reach consensus.)
- Do the people involved get along? (If so, they will probably be able to work well together.)
- Does everyone agree a problem exists? (Usually, the greater the level of agreement, the easier it will be to resolve the dilemma.)
- Is the problem recent or long-standing? (It is more difficult to change established behaviors.)
- How emotionally charged is the problem? (When feelings run high, objectivity is often lost.)

The final section, "The Caring Partnership," shows how to avoid common errors and prevent problems from occurring in the first place. It also contains more dilemmas and solutions based on questions we've been asked since the first edition, a guide to the assisted living option, and ten principles "in a nutshell" for forming a *caring partnership* with your parents.

As you try to resolve your own dilemmas, keep in mind that the more you know and the more carefully you prepare, the greater your likelihood of success.

The Context

CHAPTER ONE

کی

Harsh (and Not So Harsh) Realities

The fact that you have picked up this book probably means that you are dealing with difficult elderly parents. If you would welcome some help, you have chosen the right book.[1]

Three major assumptions will define whether this book is for you. We are making the assumption that even though your parents may be stubborn and difficult, they are still *capable* of thinking clearly and making rational decisions. That is essential if they are to be partners with you, as they should be, in making decisions that affect them.

Second, we're assuming that you and your parents are communicating. It may not be the most effective communication, but the lines are still open and you continue to interact.

Third, we're assuming that your parents have been managing their lives successfully up until now. It's just recently that something has changed. Perhaps your father insists on driving,

---

1. If your parents lack the mental capacity to make decisions, they are not simply difficult—they have special needs, and hence so do you. We recommend you look for books written specifically for caregivers of such people. For example, *The 36-Hour Day* by Nancy L. Mace and Peter V. Rabins, published as a revised edition by Warner Books in 2001, is a good starting point. In addition, an experienced geriatric physician can be a valuable source of guidance for you. If you have questions about legal competency, contact an elder law attorney for more information.

when several accidents indicate he shouldn't. Maybe your mother can't manage on her own anymore but insists she can. In any event, a disagreement has arisen over what your parents do and what you think they should do. You and they are butting heads, and an impasse has developed. You are stumped. You feel frustrated and helpless. You probably also feel a sense of urgency. Something *must* be done.

Although it's tempting to rush right in to "fix" things (to go right to the relevant dilemma in this book), first take the time to read these chapters in "The Context" section. They contain important information you need to know. Your parents' immediate problem may be just the first of many. This chapter and the next three provide the basis for approaching all the dilemmas in this book. We also intend for this information to help you approach dilemmas other than those presented here.

There are certain realities to caring for elderly parents (outlined below), and you need to pay close attention to them. They may not be easy to accept, but you can't afford to ignore them.

1. Your parents may not come around to your way of thinking.

If your parents are driving you crazy, you're probably doing battle with them over some concern you have. For example, you may dislike the way they are living or the way they are handling their money. Your parents have their own ideas, and they aren't at all the same as yours. Trying to impose your will over theirs, however, is likely to have one of four effects: (1) your parents will stop talking with you; (2) they will become even more stubborn; (3) they will comply grudgingly, with anger and resentment, and may then do their best to undermine your efforts; or (4) they will surrender to you altogether and become completely dependent on you.

Openly communicating with your parents doesn't guarantee they will see things your way or do what you want. You must be willing to give a little, to find a compromise, which may mean accepting an outcome that falls short of your wishes.

2. *Your parents have the right to make their own decisions.*

As long as your parents are capable of making decisions (once again, we assume they are), they have the right to manage their lives as they see fit. You may not always agree with their decisions or appreciate their refusal to do things as you would like. Unless their health and safety are at immediate risk, however, you have no choice but to bow out. Paradoxically, your willingness to do so may allow them to come around to your way of thinking without losing face: when people can yield without feeling foolish, they are more likely to compromise.

Contrary to popular belief, you never become "your parents' parent." Even when you become a caregiver, you are your parents' helper. Although you may have to make decisions for them, you always remain their child. Showing your respect for your parents during these times is absolutely essential if you and they are going to have a workable relationship. You can show respect by asking permission before making changes or suggestions. Instead of saying, "I'm going to arrange for grocery delivery," *ask*, "Would you like some help arranging for grocery delivery?" or "May I arrange for grocery delivery?" Your consideration will make it easier for your parents to say yes, and they won't feel obliged to pay for your help with their pride and dignity.

In some situations, you may not be able to maintain the usual balance in the parent-child relationship. If your parents' judgment is impaired, even slightly, you will have to act in their best interest, whether they like it or not. If they are rude or bullying, you may need to assert yourself strongly. Nevertheless, to the extent possible, you must show respect to get them to cooperate.

3. *Even if you can't agree, something good may come from simply talking.*

If a discussion with your parents serves no purpose other than to clarify each others' wishes and concerns, your time has been well spent. For example, if you think your widowed mother should give up her third-floor apartment, but she lets you know that she doesn't want to and can manage on her own to her satisfaction, then a fruitful exchange has taken place. Your mother knows you are concerned about her, and you know you can try again should something change.

4. Not being clear about what you want can lead to decisions no one wants.

The failure to discuss matters with each other and to get things out in the open can lead to bad decisions. If your mother agrees to move in with you because she thinks that's what *you* want, and you invite her to move in because you think that's what *she* wants, you may both end up with a "solution" that makes neither of you happy.

5. Your parents may not tell you they need help (and may deny it even if you ask).

"I didn't want to worry you" is a phrase you are likely to hear more than once. Out of pride or fear, your parents may conceal their needs and minimize their concerns. Parents don't want to be a burden on their children. Neither do they want to face their own decline. For these reasons, they often conceal their anxieties and mask their distress.

The experience of a friend of ours illustrates this point well. She visited her 75-year-old father one afternoon, and he seemed fine. But a few hours later she received a call from the hospital telling her that he had just been admitted with a mild heart attack. When she asked her father whether he had been in pain during her visit, he said yes, but he hadn't wanted to worry her.

6. Sometimes you can do little or nothing to help your parents.

Witnessing your parents' gradual decline or their struggles with major illness often creates a desire to do *something* to help. However, taking steps to make *yourself* feel better may not be in your parents' best interest. For example, insisting that they change their diet and take vitamin supplements may do little but create the illusion that you are helping them. When you confront a situation that is truly without remedy, try to remember this: patience, companionship, and caring are of far more value than hasty actions designed to relieve your anxiety. It is important to know when—as the saying goes—"to let go and let God."

7. There is almost certainly no single "right" answer to the problem you are having with your parents.

There is seldom one "right" answer to any human problem. And even if you believe you have found *the* solution, trying to force it on your parents can be downright destructive. It is far better to think in terms of alternatives, which gives everyone some breathing room. In this book, we've avoided a "single solution" approach by offering at least two or three alternatives. When a particular alternative seems more appropriate than others, we often give specific examples of things to say or do. We also teach you problem-solving methods that you can apply to *any* situation, present or future.

8. Sometimes logic doesn't count.

When it comes to caring for your elderly parents, the best decision is not necessarily the most logical, practical, or sensible one. Practicality and the ordinary standards of logic must often take a backseat to your parents' emotional needs. For example, it may make no sense logically to allow your elderly mother to keep several thousand dollars in her checking account. However, if that amount of money provides her with peace of mind, then you are making the "right" choice when you acquiesce to her leaving it there.

9. Timing is everything.

The same help, given at different times or under different circumstances, can be constructive or nonconstructive. It can even be destructive. Take, for example, your doing the dishes before you leave whenever you visit your mother. If your mother enjoys washing them after you leave because it helps relieve the loneliness she feels when you are gone, it is cruel to insist on doing them yourself. However, if her unsteady hands make this task unsafe, it is a kindness to help out, especially if your helping allows her to continue to entertain.

10. Today's solution may be out-of-date tomorrow.

When you arrive at a solution to your parents' problem, that decision may suffice for the moment. But it may well need to be reevaluated as your parents' needs change. For example, while your aging mother remains healthy, arranging for home health assistance three days a week may be sufficient to meet her needs. However, as she ages and becomes more frail, you will have to arrange for more substantial help. Eventually, you may find that she can no longer remain safely at home.

ॐ

So far we have talked only about your parents and you. But there are other realities involved when you are caring for elderly parents, having to do with siblings and other family members.

11. If a family member has never been emotionally connected to the family, don't expect a change now.

If your brother has always been emotionally remote, and if he and your parents have never gotten along well, it would be senseless to expect him to jump in and offer to help take care of them. Save your breath. Don't ask. (However, if he is the type to write a check, thinking this fulfills his familial obligations, then it may be worth asking for financial help. Still, don't be too surprised if he says no.)

Similarly, if your sister, who has always remained uninvolved with the family, agrees to help with the caregiving, don't expect her to be gracious about it. This sets you up for disappointment and places a burden on her. Ideally, everyone does things with a "good heart," but we do not live in an ideal world. Accept that your sister may be *willing* to shop for Mom but not especially *glad* to do it.

12. Old family patterns die hard.

Family roles endure. If one sibling has always fallen into the role of the "good" child, while the other has been the "exploiter" or "self-server," they will continue to behave that way even when a crisis arises with your parents. Radical personality transformations are very unlikely. Don't wait for one to occur in your family.

13. Some members of your family may not only fail to help, they may actually make your job more difficult.

Family members who are seriously disturbed may be incapable of helping—in fact, they may make the situation worse. Some are criminal in their behavior, like one man who stole money from his mother by forging checks in his deceased father's name. Others are obstructionists, like the woman who argued with her parents' physician so often that he refused to treat them anymore. If you have people like this in *your* family, do your best to work around them and minimize their involvement.

14. Your parents and your spouse or partner may have a history that can't be ignored.

If there are bad feelings between your parents and your partner or spouse, those feelings will not disappear now. And if there have been specific areas of conflict, as can happen with less traditional relationships, reactions may be even more extreme. To be blunt, if your spouse or partner can't stand your parents, he or she will probably resent the time you spend providing care for them. Or your parents may be unwilling to accept help from a partner or spouse whom they dislike. Be aware of these issues as you plan your caregiving strategies, and brace yourself for the conflicts that will inevitably occur.

The principles discussed in this chapter may not be especially pleasant to face. Nevertheless, they provide a realistic basis for your actions and decisions. It is better to look at the facts than to operate on the basis of myths and assumptions that can lead you astray. This will frustrate everyone.

In the next chapter we discuss communicating with your parents. We offer strategies to help you resolve the problems you are dealing with now and that are bound to arise in the future.

CHAPTER TWO

Talk So Your Parents Will Listen, and Listen So Your Parents Will Talk

Talking with your parents may seem like the simplest and most natural thing in the world. After all, you have spoken with them all your life. So planning for an in-depth conversation with a specific goal in mind may seem contrived. However, if you don't plan, you are likely to create unnecessary distress and may actually undermine the effects of a potentially productive conversation. For these reasons, we urge you to keep the following guidelines in mind as you prepare to talk with your parents.

1. You *set the tone of communication.*

Your emotional state affects what happens when you are talking with your parents. If you remain calm, your composure increases the likelihood that everyone will listen to each other, maintain perspective, and respond more or less logically. On the other hand, if you are panicky and begin to yell, or if you talk *at* your parents rather than *to* them, they will probably yell back, cry, or otherwise become upset. At that point, meaningful communication has come to an end.

2. *Listen more than you talk.*

In order to get your parents involved in solving the problem at hand, and in order to satisfy their needs and wishes, you have to

11

find out what your parents feel, need, and want. You can do this best by asking them questions and listening to what they say rather than by dictating what *you* think ought to be done.

3. Listen actively.

When your parents talk, don't just listen to their words. Your parents' body language may convey a very different message from what is being said to you. Tune in to the feelings they are expressing by their gestures, facial expressions, postures, use of eye contact, and tones of voice. For example, suppose your mother has just been admitted to a long term care facility. Although you know she must be distressed, she tries to reassure you (and herself) by offering comments such as, "I'm not upset" and "I don't want you to be worried about me—I'll be fine!" While her words may be comforting, the likelihood is that her level of distress is being revealed by her tone of voice. You should respond to her tone, not her words.

4. Use I-messages much of the time.

I-messages are personal statements of feelings that are free of labels, judgments, or advice. For example, here are two *I*-messages conveying concerns: "I'm very worried about your not eating, Mom," or "Dad, I get upset when you lose track of the money I give you."

   I-messages contrast strongly with *you-messages*, which often blame, shame, or judge. *You*-messages evoke angry and defensive responses from most people. Suppose your mother refuses to accept home health assistance, thereby placing more of a burden on you than you think is fair. You could berate her with a *you*-message by saying, "You're stubborn and inconsiderate," but this is only likely to hurt and anger her and create a war of wills. On the other hand, you could say, "I'm upset with this situation, Mom. It's hard for me to take care of my own children when I need to spend so much time here." Notice how this *I*-message ("*I'm* upset with this situation, Mom. . . .") doesn't blame, shame, or label. Instead, it provides information about how your mother's behavior is affecting you. There is no guarantee that this will bring about change. However, if she cares about you, she is likely to respond to your distress. If not, a more forceful *I*-message may be necessary, such as, "I need to take care of my children and cannot be your housekeeper. If you want to stay in your home, you will have to accept outside help."

5. If your parents are behaving like bullies, take a break or use you-*messages*.

When a discussion heats up and emotions run high, your parents may try to intimidate you by shouting, threatening, or being rude and offensive. *I*-messages won't have much of an effect at such times because your parents probably don't care how you feel.

You have two options at this point. One is to take a break from the conversation. Tell your parents you will not be drawn into an argument but will resume talking with them once they have calmed down. Leave the room if you can.

The other option is to confront your parents. Without being rude yourself, you can use *you*-messages to set limits. Statements such as these can put the brakes on an exchange that is running amok:

"You may not talk to me like that. I am not a child and that won't work anymore."

"You are out of line, Dad. Stop shouting!"

"You may be able to frighten others by raising your voice, but you won't get away with that with me."

It may be helpful to stand up and face your bullying parents. Standing your ground, literally, can help you get the respect you deserve.

6. Take charge if the conversation is getting out of control.

Slow your parents down if they are rushing, and calm them down if they are agitated. Hold up your hand to signal that they should stop or take a moment to gather their thoughts. Remind your parents that you are talking in order to reach an agreement, not to out-shout one another or to prove who is right and who is wrong. Take out a pad and get ready to write things down. Say something like, "I really want to understand your concerns, Mom. Tell me again, slowly, what you're worried about. I'm going to take notes." *And do it!* This action lets your parents know you are taking their words seriously and serves both to calm them and to convey respect.

7. *Avoid patronizing your parents.*

Don't underestimate your parents' capabilities. You may be providing care for your parents, but you are *not* your parents' parent. Talk straight and with respect. Although you may have to make age-related accommodations, such as talking more loudly or at a slower pace, do not treat your parents as though they were difficult or incompetent children. Doing so undermines any hope of having a meaningful dialogue with them. The same goes for withholding important or distressing information. Don't do it. It is dishonest and disrespectful.

8. *You may need to play a variety of roles.*

Five of the most important roles you may need to play at various times are these:

INFORMATION PROVIDER Your parents may need certain information to make informed decisions. Be ready to provide it. For example, if your parents are considering hiring a home health aide, give them a prescreened list of appropriate agencies you know are good. You might even offer to help arrange for someone from an agency to make an on-site visit.

FACILITATOR If your parents are upset, you may need to help them vent. Listen patiently, and accept their feelings without judgment. They will be reassured to know you understand. For example, if your mother is embarrassed about discussing her incontinence with you, you can acknowledge how difficult it is to talk about personal matters she is accustomed to keeping private.

Once she knows that *you* know how she is feeling, she may be more willing to open up and discuss solutions with you.

FACT SEEKER If there is something you need to know from your parents, you must be able to ask questions and accept answers in a straightforward and nonjudgmental way. For example, if you suspect that your elderly father has not been taking his medications, ask him about it without accusing him. When he responds, thank him for his honesty, even if his answer is not what you wanted to hear. Remember, people tend to withhold information if they fear a negative reaction.

ENCOURAGER If your parents become discouraged prematurely because they don't think their solvable problem can be resolved, they need encouragement. Remind them that others have faced similar problems and have solved them. Let them know it is important to keep trying until something works.

PEACEMAKER If your parents are living together, sometimes they won't get along well with each other. Some never did. Others are responding to stress. Regardless of the reason, arguments and conflict between them will make your job more difficult. At such times, you may need to mediate disputes to help keep the peace.

Even with these basic guidelines to help you communicate, at times you and your parents may find yourselves at a complete impasse. The next chapter provides strategies to help bring about a breakthrough.

CHAPTER THREE

❧

At an Impasse?

If you and your parents reach an impasse, don't give up. However hopeless the situation may seem, rest assured there *is* a way to break through. Often all that is needed is a way to allow your parents to change their minds without losing face. It may be that deep down they *know* you are right and have boxed themselves into a position even they can't support. You need to be sensitive, though. No one likes to hear, "I told you so," or "It's about time you listened to reason."

Below are some strategies we have gathered that can be effective in breaking the most difficult impasses. These strategies can help give your parents the room they need to change their minds willingly.

1. Alter the cast of characters.

Sometimes bringing in an outsider whom your parents trust and respect, such as a friend, a relative, or the clergy, can offer a fresh perspective that opens up new possibilities. For example, if your mother, who is resisting hiring an aide, has the utmost regard for her parish priest or her congregation's rabbi, a friendly visit and a gentle suggestion from the clergy may persuade her to try an aide. This approach will help her save face, too, because she will be able to say she is deferring to the clergy's suggestion.

Similarly, if a neighbor is pleased with an aide who helps her shop and clean, you can ask that neighbor to speak with your mother. Hearing reassurances from someone she knows may be enough to convince your mother to hire the same aide on a trial basis.

2. Allow your parents to say no now, which may enable them to say yes later.

Paradoxically, allowing your parents to voice their objections without holding back may make it possible for them to reverse themselves later. For example, suppose your parents can't manage living independently anymore but are vehemently opposed to moving into an assisted living facility. We suggest you *not* argue with them or try to convince them to move. Let them vent, and just listen. If you argue, you simply fuel their resentment or stubbornness. By not arguing, you eliminate the appearance that you are personally invested in your parents' moving—to them you will seem neutral. Taking this stance gives your parents a chance to listen to themselves and to reconsider their refusal. However, we *do* recommend you leave with them information on several facilities that might appeal to them and that would be feasible. Having this information to mull over may entice them just enough to open up to the possibility of changing their minds.

3. Find a way to satisfy your parents' wishes while giving them the help they need.

Suppose your father cares deeply for your children and has always enjoyed doing things with them. Their typical outings were always active ones—going to zoos and amusement parks. However, your father is aging, and these day trips are becoming exhausting for him. You can help him maintain contact with your children by suggesting new activities such as miniature golf or the movies, which are less strenuous for him yet still interesting to them.

4. *Take your parents' words literally in order to find some room to maneuver.*

Since a stroke left your mother disabled, your father spends all his time caring for her, and they have both become socially isolated. Your mother's doctor has urged her to spend a few hours a day at a local adult day-care center. Not only would this give your father a break, it would provide opportunities for social contact and stimulation that would benefit your mother. She likes the idea. Whenever you suggest this to your father, however, he says he is opposed to "dumping her" there. Since your father equates leaving her at day care with "dumping her," you might suggest that he remain there with her as a volunteer.

5. *Accept partial solutions.*

Sometimes you have to be willing to accept a solution that falls short of the ideal. Suppose your mother has always taken pride in cooking the entire Thanksgiving dinner by herself. However, because she has aged and the family has grown, the 25-pound turkey now needed is too heavy for her to lift safely. You prefer that she let you roast the turkey, but you know that this will upset her. Instead you can ask her to let you do the lifting while she does the roasting, thus assuring her safety while saving her pride.

6. *Turn apparent disadvantages into advantages.*

If your parents seem to hold all the aces, and you truly are unable to prevail on them to do what is in their best interest, turn your weakness into a strength. Change your approach and use a statement such as this: "Mom, Dad, there's really nothing more I can say. You have every right to do what you want. I'm absolutely powerless." Sometimes acknowledging your defeat will prompt a generous sentiment and break the impasse.

7. *Point out the consequences* for you *of your parents' behaviors.*

When your parents won't budge, let them know that their choices affect you as well as them. If your father won't take his blood pressure medication, his refusal could affect not only him but you: the burdens on you would increase dramatically if he were to have a stroke. While doctors may discharge from treatment a patient who does not follow recommendations, you can't abandon your parents for using poor judgment. However, letting them know how their refusal to be reasonable affects *you* may get them to think twice about what they are doing.

8. Show your parents they really matter to you.

Consider this well-used and often-successful option from Alcoholics Anonymous. When an alcoholic continues to deny he has a problem, his family is often advised to plan an intervention. This is a prearranged and orchestrated meeting during which caring and trusted family members and friends confront the alcoholic with personal accounts of how his drinking has affected his life and theirs. Carried out in an atmosphere of support and love, an intervention sometimes helps the alcoholic accept his need for help. The same thing can be done with your elderly parents. Although this approach may seem extreme, it is well worth considering if the situation is urgent and the impasse considerable.

9. Whisper before you shout.

When trying to resolve an impasse, first try using low-key and gentle strategies, such as providing information or sharing your concerns in the form of *I*-messages—for example, "When you don't eat properly, I really worry, Mom!" If these strategies don't work, move up to slightly more insistent ones, such as having a family meeting or arranging an intervention. As a last resort, you can notify Adult Protective Services or other government agencies. Heavy-handed options such as these are the big guns held in reserve, to be used only if all else fails.

Before you proceed, you need to realize that these dilemmas will have an impact on your *well-being. The next chapter shows you how to keep your sanity in the midst of resolving your dilemmas.*

༄

CHAPTER FOUR

S.U.R.V.I.V.E.

This chapter is not about how you can help your parents or reconcile your needs with theirs. Rather, it focuses on you, and how you can stay sane regardless of your situation. Our advice is summarized by the acronym S.U.R.V.I.V.E. The tips that follow will help you to keep your cool while trying to resolve any dilemma with your aging parents.

S tay calm.

Provided that your parents' lives and immediate safety are not at risk, your dilemma is not likely to be an emergency. You may *think* the problem is urgent when it's really not. It is important to look closely at the origins of your distress. Most often you will find the urgency comes from your concern about what others may think or from your own unrealistic expectations.

Your parents, too, may consider a problem urgent when it's not. For example, your mother, who loves to read, may be panicky about her failing eyesight. But if her ophthalmologist assures you she is not going blind, listen to the doctor. Do what you can to help Mom read (purchasing over-the-counter magnifying reading glasses may be all that is necessary), but don't let her panic sweep you up.

If you start to lose perspective, remind yourself to calm down. Walk away, literally, from a heated situation if you can. If not, take an emotional break for a few moments. Ask yourself why this problem matters so much to you and try to distinguish your needs from those of your parents.

U tilize resources.

Take advantage of the help that others offer. This is especially important if you do not live near your parents. (See *Solving Problems from Afar* on opposite page.) When people ask whether they can help, instead of saying, "That's okay, I can manage," say, "Yes, thanks!" Then tell them what they can do. The more specific you can be, the better. If you can't think of an immediate need, make a note for the future. Later you can call them and say, "I'd like to take you up on your offer to help. . . ."

Your siblings and relatives can help. So can your parents' neighbors and friends. *Ask.* If you don't ask, they may never know you need them. It is the wise person who calls for help before a situation becomes critical.

Tap into community resources as well. Volunteer drivers can take your parents on errands and to appointments. Friendly visitors can break up long days and give your parents company to look forward to. Local senior centers offer activities and classes that are both educational and enjoyable. Adult day-care facilities offer programs and activities that can help time pass and meet your parents' social needs as well.

Avoid the temptation to do it all yourself. It may seem easier at first, but in the long run it won't be. Taking everything on your shoulders is a sure way to burn out.

R espect your own limits.

Everyone's limits vary. Yours may be measured in hours ("I can only give my mother an hour of my time today") or in patience ("I will offer to help one more time; if my parents say no again, I will back off"). Whatever your limits are, respect them.

In addition, remind yourself that what is *possible* is not always *feasible*. You may want to spend every available minute taking care of your recently widowed father. But you have a hus-

Solving Problems from Afar

Taking care of your parents from afar presents special difficulties. Even a minor, short-lived problem can wreak havoc with your life. If prolonged care is required, the task may seem insurmountable. Don't despair. Think of this as simply another dilemma to be solved, carefully and rationally.

First, identify the factors to consider when deciding what to do. Next, review the options and resources that are available.

Factors to Consider

Although your impulse may be to board the first plane, consider whether you must be physically present to help your parents or whether you can arrange for appropriate care from your own home. Unless you are dealing with an acute emergency, chances are good that a few judicious calls—to your parents' physician, neighbors, nearby relatives, community resources—will suffice. It may seem uncaring not to rush off to be with your parents, but if leaving would be a hardship and if satisfactory arrangements can be made from afar, not going may be the better choice. (Beware of being hooked into thinking you must be physically present to be thought of as a "good" child.)

Next, consider the nature of the problem and how many visits will be necessary. For example, if your parents are moving to an assisted living facility and need help on moving day, a single stay of a day or two may be all that is needed. On the other hand, if your parents' situation is complicated and will require multiple visits on your part, you need to ask yourself whether you are the right person for the job.

continued on next page

Solving Problems from Afar—*continued*

Ask yourself whether—

• you can afford to make many trips, taking into account physical fatigue as well as finances;

• your family can tolerate your repeated absences;

• your job will allow it.

If you cannot answer yes to these questions, you are not the best person to furnish the care. Arrange for a relative or friend of your parents who is physically closer and less encumbered to help. If no one is available, you can hire a Geriatric Care Manager, trained in arranging for and coordinating services for the elderly. (See below.)

Resources

If your parents require ongoing care and you must arrange for it, here are several useful resources to consult.

• ELDERCARE LOCATOR, (800) 677-1116; www.eldercare.gov. A trained representative will put you in touch with the Area Agency on Aging in your parents' vicinity. This agency serves as a clearinghouse for all local sources of help. Trained staff will guide you in locating resources.

• NATIONAL ASSOCIATION OF AREA AGENCIES ON AGING, (202) 872-0888; www.n4a.org/. This is a valuable resource for anyone caring for the elderly.

• NATIONAL ASSOCIATION OF PROFESSIONAL GERIATRIC CARE MANAGERS INC., (520) 881-8008, 8 A.M. to 4:30 P.M. MST; www.caremanager.org/. This organization certifies human service professionals as Geriatric Care Managers. It also serves as a directory and referral source for them. When you tell the representative where your parents live, he or she will give you the names and contact numbers of one or more local care managers. At that point you can begin

Solving Problems from Afar—*continued*

contacting and interviewing prospective candidates. (CAUTION: This is a new field, and we have encountered some Geriatric Care Managers who lack skill and experience. Interview prospective care managers carefully, and ask for recent, verifiable references.) When you have found an acceptable candidate, be sure you understand what services will be provided and what the fees will be. Be clear about payment arrangements. Ask about progress reports, which you should receive regularly. You will need to work closely with the care manager. Be certain the person you select is someone with whom you feel comfortable. If not, keep trying until you find someone suitable.

• VISITING NURSE ASSOCIATIONS OF AMERICA, www.vnaa.org/. This organization, with a long history of providing care for home-bound individuals, can help you locate a local Visiting Nurse Association. Enter the city, state, or zip code, and you will be given a list of agencies in that area.

band, two children, and a job. You simply *can't* do all you would like. Often, good enough is just that.

Once you have announced a plan, don't go back on your word. For example, suppose you say, "I can stop by between 12 and 2 today, Dad. I have to pick up Cindy after school, so I can't stay any later." Then be sure to leave by two o'clock.

If you find yourself unable to continue doing something your parents need, find someone who can take on that activity. For example, if your mother is lonely and you can't see her as often as she would like, ask others to visit her.

V erbalize honestly.

Be sure what you say reflects what you feel. Misplaced self-sacrifice is often self-defeating. Saying, "No thanks, I'll be fine!" when you really won't be fine, will only frustrate you and confuse others.

I nclude your parents in your plans.

"My mother said she was having trouble doing her laundry," one woman complained, "so I arranged for a laundry service. Now she won't give her clothes to the man who picks them up. And *she's* angry with *me!*" By failing to talk with her mother *before* she put a plan into action, this well-meaning daughter never found out that the only trouble her mother was having was handling the heavy bottle of detergent. The lesson for you? *Always* find out your parents' view of the problem. *Always* ask whether (and how) you can help. *Always* ask permission before doing *anything*.

V alue your own feelings.

Providing care for aging parents is inherently upsetting. Expect to feel sad, angry, and frustrated at times. When you have these feelings, resist the temptation to judge yourself harshly. There are no unacceptable feelings. There are simply feelings that make sense given the situation and your relationship with your parents. For example, if you have never gotten along with your parents, don't expect to feel all right about having to help them now. Even if you have had a close or loving relationship and don't mind taking care of them, anticipate feeling sad and angry as they decline.

Be wary of people who tell you how you *should* feel. "You're lucky you have your parents to take care of." Or "Be grateful you can pay them back for all they did for you." Statements like these devalue your own feelings. Don't buy into them.

E xpect difficulties and plan for them ahead of time.

No matter how carefully you plan or how well things are going, be prepared for the possibility that something will go wrong. Your plan may be flawed in ways not initially apparent, or your parents' situation may change. In either case, take the time to look ahead and anticipate problems. Prepare backup plans.

With these tips in mind on how to S.U.R.V.I.V.E.—plus the problem-solving model in the next section—you will have the tools you need to help not only your parents but yourself as well.

The Model

✌

CHAPTER FIVE

Solve the Problems That Are Driving You Crazy

When you are faced with a situation that is driving you crazy, feelings can run strong. At times like these, you may find it difficult to stay focused on solving the problem. Thinking ahead and having a clear agenda, like the kind you would have at a well-run business meeting, will help keep you on track.

The problem-solving model we use is divided into two parts. The first part consists of six questions designed to help you clarify the problem you are confronting. The second part provides you with six steps for solving that problem. In this section of the book, we describe the basic model. In the next section we apply it to twenty-five of the most common dilemmas adult children face with their aging parents. If you find yourself in a situation we haven't covered in "The Dilemmas" section, the model below will still give you the tools you need to proceed on your own.

Clarify the Problem

No matter what problem you are facing, some basic questions must be answered *before* you attempt to solve it.

1. Does everyone agree a problem exists?

If you and your parents are going to work together to solve a problem, you must first agree there *is* a problem. Otherwise, a resolution that satisfies everyone is completely out of the question.

Sometimes recognizing a problem is easy. If your father is unable to make it through the day without falling several times, it would be difficult for anyone to deny there is a problem.

Other times, however, agreeing that a problem exists is not so easy. You may believe there is a problem, but your parents may not. For example, you have noticed changes in your mother's behavior lately that worry you—such as periodic confusion and slurred speech. Whenever you mention this to her, she says you are making too much of things. Despite her cavalier attitude, something may, indeed, be brewing. At times like this you can choose to either confront her or just wait and see.

Sometimes a problem amounts to no more than a difference of opinion. One woman, for example, had constant battles with her 91-year-old mother, who insisted on eating large quantities of ice cream and very few fruits and vegetables. The mother's doctor was satisfied with her health, weight, and diet; and the mother was happy eating the foods she enjoyed. The only "problem" was that her diet didn't match what her daughter thought was appropriate.

2. How urgent is the problem, really?

True crises, involving life and death, are acted upon immediately because they have to be. They seldom last long enough to drive you crazy. When confronting a problem that *seems* urgent, first ask yourself, What will happen if I do nothing? Chances are the answer is, Nothing awful—at least not right away. Follow the principle that guides physicians: "First, do no harm." Allow yourself some time to think.

How long should you wait before doing something? It depends. Sometimes you can't afford to wait long. For example, if your father's driving makes him a daily hazard, you will not want to wait until he injures or kills someone before confronting him. Your wait period for this situation will be as short as possible, just the amount of time needed to come up with a workable plan.

On the other hand, if your father has a problem that is less urgent, you may have to take a wait-and-see approach. For example, suppose your father is managing to live on his own despite some loss of vision. You think he will be better off in an assisted living facility, but he doesn't agree. He knows his way around his home by feel, and he can take care of his basic needs. Since he is able to cope at present, your solution at this time is to wait. Plan to intervene only when his vision has deteriorated to the point where he can no longer manage his day-to-day activities. No matter how well intended, any premature action on your part—such as forcing your father to relocate before he wants to or insisting he come live with you—will almost certainly cause more problems than it solves.

3. What is behind your parents' problematic behaviors?

To counter your parents' behaviors, you have to understand what is behind them. Your elderly father's refusal to stop driving, for example, is probably tied in to his self-esteem and self-reliance. If he were to stop driving, his world would shrink, and he would become dependent on others. Given how important driving is in his life, his apparent stubbornness makes sense.

To even admit that a problem exists, your parents must be able to accept that they are aging and recognize the limitations this brings. If they cannot do this, their only alternative is to deny that anything has changed. If you could look inside your parents' subconscious minds, the ideas below are what you would probably find:

If I don't admit a need, then it doesn't exist.

If I don't accept help, then I don't need it.

This kind of reasoning, illogical though it may be, is very common and is usually in operation when resistance seems irrational.

For stubborn parents, accepting help may mean one or more of the following:

They must admit to themselves that they are declining physically. For example, a woman unable to walk safely may refuse to use a wheelchair because to do so will be to concede she is no longer able to get around on her own.

They must acknowledge that they can no longer do things as well as they used to. Your parents may refuse to accept a home health aide because it will mean acknowledging that neither they nor their family are able to manage their needs any longer.

They must face the fact that something may be wrong with them. A woman may refuse to see a physician although it is obvious she needs to, because if she does, she will no longer be able to deny her serious health problems.

Below are some common psychological defenses your parents will use to deny the existence of a problem. Once you learn to recognize these defenses and to respect the vulnerability and fear they cover up, your efforts to help are more likely to succeed.

Denial is a declaration that "there is no problem." Only information that supports this perception is admissible. Information that contradicts it is simply ignored or brushed aside. A man refused to take his wife to a doctor even though she was showing clear signs of dementia, including memory loss and bizarre behaviors. Why? Because he was driven by fear. As long as he could continue to believe that nothing had changed, that his wife's condition was not serious, and that neither she nor he needed help, there *was* no problem.

Minimization is a partial denial. When your parents minimize a problem, they are pretending to themselves that their condition or the situation they find themselves in isn't serious. They will make statements like these:

"I didn't tell you about my chest pains because they weren't so bad; I didn't want to worry you."

"The money I gave to that man from the charity organization wasn't enough to get upset about."

Saying things like this provides hollow reassurance that troubling events are less serious than they really are.

Rationalization involves giving reasonable-sounding explanations without taking responsibility. When your mother tells you she fell "because the floor was slippery," she is omitting the fact that her unsteady gait made her vulnerable. When your father says he had an accident "because the other drivers were going too fast," he is overlooking the ways his driving may have contributed to the accident. Face-saving, after-the-fact explanations make it unnecessary to look at the realities your parents want to ignore.

Your parents' decisions are a product of their thinking and reflect their needs and values as well. Decisions that seem illogical make more sense when you look beneath the surface to see the mental steps that your parents followed. (*Demystifying "Illogical" Decisions* on the next page demonstrates such a process.)

4. What's hooking you?

This part of clarifying the problem can be difficult. You aren't likely to become frustrated by a problem unless it's hooking you. For example, if you are angry that your parents will not live with you, ask yourself whose needs would be met by their doing so— yours or theirs?

We don't mean to suggest that the problems we are writing about aren't distressing. They are, especially when they concern health, safety, and quality of life. But when the degree of your distress is out-of-line with the urgency of the situation, something is hooking you and clouding your objectivity.

The most common caregiver hooks are these:

THE RESCUE HOOK Some children feel they can, and must, make everything all right for their parents. For example, a daughter might be unable to accept her parent's terminal illness. As a result, she runs herself ragged and neglects her own needs to find a cure. When she fails, she feels anxious and guilty.

Sometimes an adult child feels compelled to save her parents from themselves. A daughter of alcoholic parents might

Demystifying "Illogical" Decisions

Many of the decisions made by elderly parents make no sense at all to their children. However, if you try to understand your parents' perspective, their choices will make a lot more sense.

When your parents (or anyone else) make a decision, they go through a multistep process that occurs so rapidly they are often unaware of it.

- In the first step, your parents identify their options. (We can go to Florida for the winter, or we can stay home.)
- In the next step, they determine the consequences of each option and how they feel about them. (If we go to Florida, it will be warm, and we enjoy walking in the sun. However, even a small hotel room will be expensive, and money is tight this year. We would be far from the children, and we'd miss them. And the last few winters here were pretty mild, so we were able to get out fairly often.)
- Finally, the pros and cons are weighed and a decision is made. (We'd probably be better off staying home this year. If it really is unpleasant, we'll go away next winter.)

Notice that being close to family is more important to your parents than being warm. They also take into consideration a continued warming trend with the weather. Your thought process, on the other hand, might be completely different. You would rather be warm than see your relatives, and you believe this winter will be a killer. You probably think your parents are crazy for staying up north.

If you go through this process with your parents' perspective in mind and examine every decision your parents make in terms of their beliefs, needs, values, and priorities, you may find that their seemingly illogical choices are not so crazy after all.

sacrifice her marriage, her health, and her career to help her parents, even though they make no serious effort to help themselves.

THE GOOD-CHILD HOOK If you and your siblings have been rivals for your parents' affections, one of you is likely to take on the role of the "good" child. When disagreements arise over how to handle a problem, the "good" child becomes the parents' advocate and tries to protect them from the "bad" sibling. For example, if your "bad" brother wants to admit your elderly mother to a nursing home, you might say, "Don't worry, Mom, I won't let him put you away." When something like this happens, your parents' needs take a backseat to the rivalries between you and your siblings. (Ironically, your parents may unconsciously pit you against each other to cast you in your familiar roles.)

THE WHAT-WILL-OTHERS-THINK HOOK Sometimes the compulsion to help your parents comes from your concern about what others might think. For example, if your parents are safe and happy living in their small apartment under less than optimal conditions, there is no need for you to insist on changes. It is your fear that others will consider you irresponsible for "allowing" your parents to live this way that is interfering with your judgment.

5. Who must be included in problem-solving discussions?

When trying to resolve any serious dilemma, everyone whom the dilemma may affect must be involved, especially those who have veto power or the power to sabotage your plans and make your life difficult. Even siblings who have had minimal involvement in your parents' care should be asked to participate.

It is tempting to exclude certain people from problem-solving discussions, since the fewer people involved, the easier it is sometimes to reach an agreement. However, anyone with a stake in the outcome (financial or otherwise) or whose cooperation you will depend on must be included. If they are not, they are likely to second-guess you, undermine your plan, or accuse you of manipulating the situation for your own convenience or personal gain. This includes such individuals as your parent's spouse, domestic partner, or significant other—anyone who can either legally challenge your decisions or simply say, "No, I will not," or "No, I will not allow it."

It is especially important to gather everyone who is involved when your parents are likely to oppose a decision. It is common for elderly parents, sensing dissension, to rely on a divide-and-conquer strategy. Frightened and backed into a corner, they may well exploit a lack of unanimity in an effort to get their way. If they succeed, they are the ones who may suffer.

6. What is your goal?

To formulate your goal, decide what a successful outcome will look like. In other words, if you accomplish your goal, what will be different? For example, suppose your mother has always cleaned her own house. Lately, however, you notice the house smells funny, and dust is accumulating on the furniture. Your goal in this situation is to get your mother help—probably with house cleaning—without damaging her self-esteem.

Solve the Problem

Once you have explored and answered the six questions designed to help you clarify your problem, the next step is to solve the problem.

1. Decide on the needs your solution must satisfy.

Any sound decision you make must meet certain criteria, or needs. For example, when you buy a car, you decide whether you need a sedan or a convertible, a manual or an automatic transmission, and so on. In the same way, every decision you make regarding your parents must satisfy specific needs. The more carefully you outline these needs, the more satisfied everyone is likely to be. Typical needs to consider include the following:

SAFETY AND HEALTH Does the solution ensure that your parents are not placed at risk?

ACCEPTABILITY Is the solution acceptable to your parents? You can't count on their cooperation unless they find the decision satisfactory. If at all possible, the solution should also be satisfactory to the others involved in the dilemma or at least lend itself to compromise.

PRACTICALITY Is the solution realistic? Is it affordable, both financially and emotionally?

Not all needs carry the same weight. Safety and health, for example, are more important than either of the others. Keep this in mind when formulating solutions.

2. Come up with a few possible solutions.

Begin this process by taking into account the facts of the situation, your parents' needs and wishes, and your own. Then identify as many realistic options as possible that can help resolve the dilemma, including those that represent compromises or steps on the way to your goal. Suppose your father had knee surgery, and his doctor told him he had to have physical therapy so that his knee could heal properly. Despite knowing this, your father refuses to pay for a taxi to take him to the therapist. One solution might be to arrange for physical therapy at home. Another might be to pay for the taxi yourself. A third solution might be for you to drive him to therapy.

3. Analyze your choices and select the best solution.

One way to do this is by constructing a chart like the one on page 39. (You may have used such charts when choosing a new appliance or a computer; they work just as well when making decisions about your parents.)

- The first step is to formulate a question that clearly states what your goal is. For example, if your brother won't help take care of your parents, your question will be, "How can I get my brother to lend a hand?"

- Next, down the left side of the page and in order of importance, list the needs your solution must meet (described in step 1, pages 36-37). Then, across the top, write your possible solutions (described in step 2, page 37). If the dilemma you are facing is not an emergency, your first possible solution always should be to "do nothing." Including this option will make you stop and think about whether doing something will really make things better.

- Next, fill in the rest of the chart by writing *yes, no,* or an appropriate comment in the boxes to indicate whether or to what degree each solution meets the need. If specific conditions must be met for your solution to work, say so. Similarly, if you need information before you can judge the worth of your solution, remind yourself to get it.

To better understand how the chart works, here is an example:

Suppose your elderly mother, who lives in an apartment in a nearby city, has been managing well on her own since she was widowed several years ago. Over the past few months, however, you and your two brothers have noticed there is an unusual scarcity of food in her house. The food you do see is an odd assortment. Her kitchen cabinets hold chips, dehydrated soups, and bags of microwave popcorn. In her refrigerator are some cold cuts, mushrooms, and sliced bread, but no milk or juice. When you asked her about this, she shrugged and said that it is what she likes to eat.

While watching your mother move about her kitchen, you have also noticed she has difficulty lifting things. She sets the table by carrying dishes from the cabinet one-by-one, instead of stacking them and bringing a few at a time. She has trouble lifting pots and pans. It seems evident that her inability to carry heavy items accounts for her not buying milk and canned goods. You are concerned about her inadequate diet but don't want to insult her or put her in a position of having to deny her need for help. Going shopping is an important part of her routine, and getting out of the house is good exercise, so you don't want to start doing the shopping for her.

Any solution you come up with must preserve your mother's dignity yet not impose too great a burden on you or your brothers. (If your mother were too frail to shop at all, or if her judgment were impaired, her needs and your solutions would be quite different.)

You come up with several solutions that can help your mother: (1) she can shop at the supermarket and have them deliver her groceries; (2) you and your brothers can share responsibility for taking her shopping by doing so in weekly shifts; or (3) you can hire someone to take her shopping, who can carry the groceries to her apartment and help her put them away.

When you record the goal, the situation's needs, and the solutions you came up with, the chart looks like this:

GOAL: How can we help Mom shop for items she can't carry by herself?

NEEDS	POSSIBLE SOLUTIONS			
	Do nothing	Have the super-market deliver your mother's groceries	Have you or your brothers take your mother shopping	Hire someone to take your mother shopping
Must provide your mother with needed groceries	no	yes, if delivery service is available	yes	yes
Must safeguard your mother's independence	yes	yes, since she will continue to shop for herself	need to find out how she feels about this	need to find out how she feels about this
Must be realistic in terms of time and expense	yes	most likely	need to check with your brothers	need to check into expense and availability

Looking at this analysis, doing nothing is not a solution if your mother is to get the groceries she needs. The best solution seems to be having her groceries delivered, since that keeps her in full control of her shopping.

It is often a good idea to have all the needed facts on hand (in this case, availability and cost of the delivery service, and an idea about who will pay for it) before making your pitch. Proving to your parents that your plan is realistic and workable may be what it takes to get them to agree. In other cases, it may make more sense to change the order of operations and propose an idea to your parents first rather than spend time and effort getting information or securing the cooperation of other people only to have your parents oppose the idea.

4. Conduct a "Murphy's Law" analysis.

Murphy's Law states that "anything that can go wrong will go wrong." Conducting a Murphy's Law analysis means anticipating problems that can arise with your preferred solution and formulating strategies to avoid them.

In the example, what if your mother decided she didn't feel safe opening her door to a delivery person? Your solution might then be to have her tip in advance, and have the person ring her bell and leave the groceries. Suppose your mother didn't hear the bell when the groceries arrived? You might install a louder bell or a flashing light so your mother is certain to know someone is at the door. You need to plan for contingencies and take whatever steps you can to reduce the chance of things going wrong.

5. Carry out your plan.

Once one solution is found to be clearly better than the others, plan how you want to approach your parents. Getting their cooperation is necessary for any change to occur. Present your plan in the most persuasive way possible, remembering to use appropriate *I*-messages to convey your concerns. If you want to present several possibilities, you might write them down so your parents can consider them at their leisure. Bear in mind, however, that the more options you present, the more confusing the situation will be for your parents. Once you have their agreement on a plan, ask for their involvement in working to bring it into effect.

In the example, if your mother accepts the idea of home delivery, ask whether she would like your help arranging for it. Also ask her to make a shopping list, including the items she has avoided buying. If the arrangement calls for her to shop at the store in person, offer to go with her when she sets up the delivery service, as well as the first time she tries it out. If she would prefer to phone in her order, make certain she knows whom to call, and offer to help her the first time she does it.

6. Evaluate your progress.

There are two main ways to determine whether your plan is working. First, does everything *look* in order? Although what you see can be deceptive, looking around is still a good place to start. In the example, you can check the cabinets and refrigerator to see whether the expected foods are there. Does your mother look healthy? Does she seem to be maintaining her weight?

Next, what do you *hear*? Listen for both what is said and what is not said. Sometimes in order to avoid being a bother, parents gloss over dissatisfactions. Statements like "Everything's fine" and "Don't worry about me" often signal veiled concerns. This is when you need to actually *ask* specific questions. In the example, you might ask your mother directly whether she thinks the plan is working. Are her groceries being delivered promptly? Has she had trouble knowing when the delivery person is at her door? Let her know that you are asking these questions because you want to make sure everything is going as planned for her.

If minor problems come up, find ways to take care of them. Consider it a fine-tuning of your solution. However, if more serious problems appear, you may need to consider the other options from your chart. For example, if home delivery is the option you agreed on, but your mother consistently complains that her groceries are not delivered promptly or that she is sent the wrong items, you will need to try a different solution.

NOTE: Appendix B provides a sample worksheet you can use or copy to make notes for your own situations.

Three Suggestions for Using the Model

ADAPTATIONS To get the most out of this problem-solving model, adapt it to your own circumstances. Only you know—

- your parents—their histories, temperaments, and needs;
- the specifics of your current dilemma;
- the personalities and behaviors of your family of origin and your current family, and the relationships among them;
- the ideas that are likely to be accepted and acted on.

Use this knowledge to find the solution that best fits your own cast of characters. Apply the model flexibly. For example, if we suggest that you include all your siblings in the problem-solving discussion, but you know your brother's presence will prevent the discussion from even getting started, then meet without him.

PARTIAL SOLUTIONS As we discussed in chapter 3, at times you may need to accept partial solutions (see page 19). You may also find yourself confronted with a multi-phased problem. You can reduce that complex problem to smaller units or "mini-dilemmas," which can be tackled separately by using the model. For example, suppose your mother's back problem has caused her to withdraw from her friends, abuse medication, and stop shopping and cleaning. Using the model, treat each concern as a separate dilemma, beginning with the one that seems most urgent. Even if you can't solve everything right away, a small improvement is better than none at all, and it may be the first step toward a more complete resolution.

REVISIONS Where elderly parents are concerned, nothing is set in stone. Be prepared to revise and rethink your solution as changes occur in your parents' health or finances, or in your own life. It is better to think of any resolution you arrive at as the *start* of a process rather than as a final and unchanging product.

Now that you are equipped with this problem-solving model, you can approach not only the dilemmas presented in the following pages but also any others encountered in your life as the child of aging parents.

The Dilemmas

సౌ

My father can no longer drive safely, but he refuses to stop.

Situation

Your father is an 87-year-old retired teacher. At 16, he became the primary driver for his parents, to whom automobiles remained a mystery all their lives. Your mother does not drive. Many years ago when she wanted to learn, your father discouraged her. Your parents, who live in a small private home, use their car to visit friends and relatives and to do the weekly food shopping. Your father prides himself on his driving record. Even though he has had several minor accidents over the past few years, he maintains that none were his fault. He disparages old drivers and does not consider himself one of them.

Recently, his neighbors have been calling you to complain about his driving. They are concerned that he doesn't look behind him when he backs up, and they report that he has nearly caused several accidents. In addition, he has sideswiped two cars (which he claims were parked where they didn't belong). When you and your two sisters suggested to your father that it might be time to give up driving, he reacted angrily, accusing the neighbors and you of making a fuss over nothing. Besides, he says, he's not ready to be put out to pasture.

Clarify the Problem

1. Does everyone agree a problem exists?

Although you, your two sisters, and your father's neighbors certainly believe there is a problem, your father doesn't agree. He is licensed and therefore legally entitled to drive. It would be difficult to establish that he is an incompetent driver, because objectively he has not done anything—yet—that is worse than what many younger drivers do. However, it is becoming impossible to ignore the situation.

2. How urgent is the problem, really?

Nothing terrible has happened to date. Nevertheless, unless your father is very lucky, it is only a matter of time before something more serious occurs. Therefore, *some* action needs to be taken at the present time.

3. What is behind your father's problematic behavior?

It is important for you and your sisters to understand the reasons your father will not stop driving voluntarily. Only then can you appreciate what quitting will mean for him.

Consider the role that driving has played in your father's life. Imagine how proud he must have felt as a youngster to be so indispensable to his parents. Once married, his role as driver again allowed him to be centrally important. (In discouraging your mother from learning to drive, he was—perhaps unconsciously—guaranteeing his status and her dependence on him.) These facts give you a sense of how important driving is to his self-concept and self-esteem.

You also need to see your father at 87 as a member of a generation very different from yours. When he started driving, cars were relatively new and certainly not owned by everyone. People went "motoring" just for the pleasure of it. Because many people did not drive, someone who *could* drive had special importance. People worked on their cars themselves and were proud of them.

There was a cult around driving. Your father's roles as driver and man of the house have given him a standing he is reluctant to surrender.

Finally, think about how dependent today's society is on automobiles. There are fewer opportunities available to those who do not drive. Remember as well the rite of passage you experienced when you learned to drive. Your world opened up to you. And it was the same for your father. Asking him to stop driving now is like asking an adult to become a child again. Additionally, once your father stops driving, many aspects of his life as an individual, and your parents' life as a couple, will change for the worse. Your parents' outings help structure their days and make each week meaningful. Quitting will mean limiting their freedom and mobility. For your father it will also mean a loss of self-esteem, security, and sense of belonging to society—hence, his reference to being "put out to pasture."

4. What's hooking you?

In addition to legitimate concerns for your parents' safety, other factors may be at work. You may feel that your father's behavior is a reflection on you; you may be embarrassed when the neighbors call you to complain about him. You may also fear that they will regard you as irresponsible if you allow this situation to continue. In this and similar situations, you need to set aside your *own* involvement to get an accurate read on the situation and to determine its urgency. If the neighbors hadn't said anything, would you still feel as concerned?

5. Who must be included in problem-solving discussions?

You, your sisters, and your parents need to be involved. Your sisters and you need to agree on how to proceed and how to ensure that your parents will be able to shop and visit friends and relatives. Your father must be involved since it is his driving that is in question. Finally, because your mother almost certainly has an opinion about your father's driving, she should also be involved in the discussion. Her role is important here, because she may serve as an ally (if she agrees with you) to help persuade your father. Be sure you don't enlist her support, however, by going behind your father's back. That poses too great a risk for creating dissension between your parents.

6. What is your goal?

You hope to convince your father to give up driving altogether—or failing that, to limit it dramatically—so that he no longer runs the risk of endangering himself or anyone else.

Solve the Problem

1. Decide on the needs your solution must satisfy.

Your solution must sharply reduce or eliminate the likelihood that your father will injure himself or anyone else as a result of his driving. At the same time, you must protect his feelings as much as possible and come up with a solution that he can accept, if not like. Your mother, too, must find the solution acceptable. Finally, it must provide your parents with alternative transportation while being realistic and not asking too much of family members who are involved.

2. Come up with a few possible solutions.

One solution is to convince your father to give up driving completely. Another is to urge him to accept limitations if you feel he could drive safely with restrictions. For example, if his night vision is poor, perhaps he will agree to limit his driving to daylight hours. If backing up is his main problem (as it often is for elderly people who have difficulty twisting around), your mother can help double-check for traffic with him.

If your father absolutely refuses to give up or limit his driving because he feels no need to, a different negotiated solution might be possible. Convince him to have a physical and to be retested by the Department of Motor Vehicles (DMV). If he passes the physical and the DMV test, you will stop pestering him (although you will still want to monitor his driving). If he doesn't pass either the physical or the DMV test, he must agree to the state's decision, which would most likely be to impose restrictions on his driving or to revoke his license.

You can enlist the help of his physician if you wish. Let the physician know you believe your father's limitations as a driver put him at risk. Provide documentation in the form of accident reports, neighbors' complaints, etc., and request an examination. Physicians who treat elderly patients perform these exams quite frequently, and many elderly people accept their doctor's judgment. Such an outcome provides them with a way to save face because they can say to themselves, quite accurately, that they cannot drive because of "doctor's orders."

If your father won't accept any of these approaches and continues to place himself and others at risk, you may have to use a last-resort strategy. It is not one we normally recommend, but it may be unavoidable. You can report your father to the DMV. The agency will then revoke his license pending an investigation and a retesting. There are two significant risks associated with this admittedly extreme action. First, your father will have to cope, abruptly, with the loss of something he values very highly. Anger and depression may occur as he comes to terms with this loss. Second, your action may well undermine your relationship with your father, since he will blame you for taking the decision to drive out of his hands. Although these consequences are undesirable, they are preferable to allowing him to harm himself or an innocent party. (See *Older Drivers: Resources and Information* on page 51.)

3. Analyze the choices and select the best solution.

(See chart on next page.)

Convincing your father to stop driving or to limit it voluntarily is the most desirable solution, since it accomplishes your purposes without resorting to strong-arm tactics.

GOAL: How can I get my father to stop driving?

	POSSIBLE SOLUTIONS			
NEEDS	Do nothing	Convince your father to stop or limit his driving voluntarily	Convince your father to abide by the results of a physical and a DMV retesting	Report your father to the DMV
Must sharply reduce or eliminate your father's driving	no	yes	probably	probably
Must respect his self-esteem and allow him to save face	yes	yes, if carefully thought out and implemented	probably	no
Must be acceptable to your mother	uncertain	probably	probably	probably not
Must provide transportation adequate to meeting your parents' needs	yes	yes, if prearranged	yes, if prearranged	initially, no
Must be realistic	no	yes	yes	yes

4. Conduct a Murphy's Law analysis.

Assuming your father *does* agree to limit or stop his driving, you and your sisters will have committed yourselves to providing or arranging for backup transportation. You will need to be prepared for the possibility that your arrangements may not work and, therefore, will have to be renegotiated.

If making the transition to alternative transportation overwhelms your parents, resulting in fewer social contacts and a deterioration of their quality of life, you will need to intervene and help them with their plans.

Another possibility is that your father promises to limit his driving but does not do so. You will have no choice then but to

---

Older Drivers: Resources and Information

Department of Motor Vehicles (DMV) officials in every state are aware of the problem of older drivers. Most states have procedures for such cases as your parent's. Visit or contact your local DMV office for more information. Listed below are additional resources.

AARP, (888) 687-2277, 7 A.M. to midnight Eastern time; www.aarp.org/ is a good source of information. The 55 ALIVE/Mature Driving driver-improvement course is a helpful AARP offering.

AMERICAN AUTOMOBILE ASSOCIATION FOUNDATION FOR TRAFFIC SAFETY, (202) 638-5944, www.aaafts.org/ can provide additional information in the form of brochures and videos.

DRIVERS.COM is a Web site devoted to driving and driver behavior. At www.drivers.com/topic/10 you can find information and helpful links for older drivers and their families.

---

increase the pressure. Insist that he take and abide by the results of a physical and a DMV retesting. If the results indicate he should not drive, but he continues to drive, you will have to report him to the DMV.

5. Carry out your plan.

Two steps are required to get your father to stop or limit his driving voluntarily. The first is to get him to acknowledge that there *is* a problem with his driving. The second is to show him that his needs, and those of your mother, will continue to be met even after he no longer drives.

One way to convince your father that a problem exists is by presenting the facts in a way that is sensitive to his feelings. You might say something like this: "Dad, I know you've been driving since you were 16 and have always been proud of your skills. And I know that you and Mom enjoy getting out to run errands and to visit. But yesterday Mrs. Jones called me, very upset, and said that you sideswiped her car while you were backing out of the driveway. I know you said you will pay for the damage, but this kind of thing never used to happened before, and I would feel awful if you hurt yourself or one of the neighbors. I imagine *you're* upset about this, too. Can we talk about what you think is going on? We really need to find a way to keep this from happening again."

By confronting your father with the facts, you are making it hard for him to deny that there has been a change in his driving ability. He might be defensive, but your stance that these changes represent a departure from his previously safe record is hard to ignore.

Before approaching your parents, prepare adequately. Learn how they use their car and how it keeps them in touch with the world at large. You and your sisters can then provide your father with alternatives, such as hiring a driver, using a taxi or public transportation, or letting you and your siblings share the driving. Your father might prefer to pay for his rides, or you and your sisters could share the cost. If the cost of a driver or taxi service becomes a point of contention, remind your father what it costs to own and operate his car, including gasoline, maintenance, and insurance. When all of these are considered, your options may seem more reasonable to him.

6. Evaluate your progress.

Initially, you and your sisters will have to stay on top of things and work out the rough edges. If your plan is not working—if your father is continuing to drive more than he should, or if your parents' emotional and social needs are not being met—you will have to arrange for a family meeting and rethink how to proceed. (See *Family Meetings* on pages 65–66.) This will involve finding out why the plan is failing. Why, for example, is your father continuing to drive even though he promised not to? When you know the answers to questions like this, you can find appropriate remedies.

Whatever you decide, you will probably need to make adjustments as your parents' needs change. This is especially true if your plan initially has your father driving on a limited basis. However, once he no longer equates driving with being seen as a worthwhile and vital person, he will probably be more likely to accept changes.

ॐ

My mother antagonizes
her aide.

Situation

You have always had a stormy relationship with your mother, who is now 84 years old. Even after you reached adulthood, she continued to bully you and be critical of most of the things you do. Your father, whom she treated similarly, died 10 years ago. Since his death, you have visited your mother regularly and have tried to overlook her critical attitude.

Your mother has managed well on her own, but last year it became apparent that she needed help with her shopping and cleaning. You helped her for several months, but eventually the time commitment became too great and you realized you could not continue. You told that to your mother and convinced her to allow an aide to come in three mornings a week to help out.

Within two weeks, the aide quit, claiming that your mother was impossible to work for. You spoke with your mother, who said that the aide was unpleasant and wouldn't do as she was told. Your mother also complained that she didn't know why you couldn't take care of her as you had done previously. You told her again that you were no longer able to and now you would have to hire another aide. You did find another aide, but it was the same story. Within weeks, the aide quit.

Clarify the Problem

1. Does everyone agree a problem exists?

You and your mother are both aware that a problem exists, but you each see the problem differently. From your perspective, the problem is that your mother's behavior is driving away aides, thus making it impossible for her to receive needed help. From her perspective, the problem is twofold: (1) the aides do not live up to her standards, and (2) you are unwilling to take care of her yourself.

2. How urgent is the problem, really?

This problem is an urgent one. Since your mother cannot shop or clean on her own, someone needs to. If you capitulate to her demands and fill this role, your resentment will take a toll on your physical and emotional well-being. Yet you cannot continue to hire new people only to have them leave after a few days. A better solution has to be found, and as quickly as possible.

3. What is behind your mother's problematic behavior?

Although your mother has not explicitly stated she does not want an aide, her behavior indicates she is opposed to the arrangement. Her critical, unpleasant manner, which has driven away the aides, may be her way of telling you she doesn't want strangers taking care of her. She may also enjoy having you take care of her, even if she cannot express the enjoyment, and she may fear that if you don't *have* to visit, you won't.

4. What's hooking you?

Your mother is resisting your best efforts to meet her needs. Any attempt to reason with her has come to a dead end. Your frustration with her behavior toward the aides, together with her history of mistreating you, may well be interfering with your efforts. Only by staying emotionally detached can you hope to find a solution to this problem. In other words, *expect* her to criticize your efforts. *Expect* her to be dissatisfied with the help she gets. If you can stand firm and face your own discomfort at being called bad, uncaring, or anything else she throws your way, you will more likely be able to persist in arranging for the help she needs.

5. Who must be included in problem-solving discussions?

The only people who need to discuss this problem are you and your mother.

6. What is your goal?

Your goal is to see to it that your mother gets the help she needs, without overtaxing yourself, so she can stay in her home. She does not have to *like* it, but she needs to *accept* it.

Solve the Problem

1. Decide on the needs your solution must satisfy.

Your mother needs a clean house and food to eat. You need to stop providing direct care.

2. Come up with a few possible solutions.

One solution is to find an aide who can stand up to your mother or ignore her. (Who knows? Over time, your mother might come to enjoy the company of someone she can't frighten off.)

If you cannot find anyone suitable, you can hire a cleaning service and arrange for delivery of her groceries. This solution will meet your mother's basic needs while muting the effect of her critical ways. It will not provide your mother with companionship, but that is not your primary concern at this time.

If your mother refuses to allow anyone to come in to clean and refuses to allow delivery of her groceries, you can propose a temporary compromise, whereby you do one task, such as the shopping, but someone else is hired to do the other. If that works, you have bought some relief for the time being and can work on another solution down the road.

Regardless of which plan you choose, you can reassure

your mother that you will continue to see her on a regular basis, even if your visits only provide company. Although she may deny that your presence is important to her, this assurance may allow her to accept a solution she would otherwise reject.

If your mother refuses to cooperate entirely, you have no choice but to tell her that she is on her own. Let her know you will look in on her periodically and if you feel that her health or safety is at risk, you will call Adult Protective Services and have her put in a protective environment. (See *Adult Protective Services* on page 70.) It is not a pretty situation, but she needs limits placed on her behavior, and there are not many options.

3. Analyze the choices and select the best solution.

GOAL: How can I get my mother the help she needs?

NEEDS	POSSIBLE SOLUTIONS				
	Do nothing	Hire an aide who can deal with critical and antagonistic behaviors	Hire a cleaning service and arrange for grocery delivery	Do one of the tasks and hire someone else to do the other	Monitor your mother and notify Adult Protective Services if necessary
Must provide your mother with food and a clean house	no	yes, with the added benefit of companionship	yes, but without the added benefit of companionship	yes, with the added benefit of companionship	yes, if Adult Protective Services intervenes
Must give you relief from hands-on caregiving	no	yes	yes	partial relief	yes

The best solution is to hire an aide experienced in dealing with difficult seniors who will not be scared away by your mother.

4. Conduct a Murphy's Law analysis.

The success of your plan depends on finding a person who will be able to cope with your mother. However, you may not find someone confident and experienced enough to deflect her abuse, or you may find someone who responds to your mother's criticism by being nasty and abusive in return. If either of these happens, you have no choice but to try the other possible solutions you have identified until one of them works.

5. Carry out your plan.

To implement your plan, interview various agency administrators until you find someone with the maturity, judgment, and experience to appreciate your dilemma and to assign someone likely to succeed with your mother. Then interview each candidate and forewarn him or her about your mother's behaviors. Evaluate the candidate's suitability by the responses you get. Ask specific questions. For example, "If my mother called you names, what would you do?" Reject candidates who cannot come up with responses indicating the maturity and detachment necessary to handle your mother.

Once you have chosen someone, reassure your mother that you will continue to visit. Be sure to be present when the aide arrives for the first time and at least a few times thereafter. Make clear that the aide has your full support.

Since being a critical bully has allowed your mother to "call the shots" in the past, you are not likely to change her basic temperament now. However, you must do your best to change the way she actually behaves with others. There are two ways to attempt this. One is to point out the consequences of her not changing: if she doesn't accept help from others, you yourself won't provide it, and she will be unable to live independently any longer. The other is to point out the impact of her behavior on others. For example, using the principles of communication discussed in chapter 2, you might say something like, "Mother, we need to talk about why Marie and Ellen quit. I know when you've told *me* that the kitchen floor doesn't look clean after I have tried my best, I've felt like never coming back again. I suspect that Marie and Ellen felt the same way, and that's why they left."

While this gentle confrontation isn't likely to bring about an instant transformation, your comment may start a thought process by which your mother may begin to temper her behavior.

Tell your mother and the aide that if problems develop between the two of them, they should first try to resolve their disagreements themselves. If they are not able to do so, let them know that you will try to help.

Periodically, let the aide know you appreciate his or her endurance and willingness to tolerate your mother's critical attitude. As time goes on, your mother is likely to come to accept both the help and the company, perhaps even enjoy them, even if she never admits it.

6. Evaluate your progress.

You will know soon enough if things are not going well. Expect that your mother will complain no matter what solution you choose. On the other hand, you will know you have succeeded if she is getting the help she needs and you are spared the hardship of providing it all yourself.

~~~

My brother and sister won't offer to help take care of Mom and Dad.

Situation

You are a 35-year-old, fifth-grade teacher, married, with two children, 7 and 5 years old. You have been helping your elderly parents, who live 20 minutes away from you, for the past two years by shopping for them twice a week and dropping in on Saturdays to help with the housework. You are growing tired of doing this, however, and are becoming resentful. In addition, your husband and children are beginning to complain about all the time you spend away from home. You would like more time to be with them and to be able to attend more of your youngsters' after-school and weekend activities. You also want more time to relax.

Your brother and sister, both older than you and also living nearby, have never offered to help, although they have complimented you on your patience and have acknowledged your hard work. Your sister enjoys your parents' company but talks constantly about the demands of her job as a marketing analyst and the long hours she has to work. Your brother, a stockbroker, has never been close to either parent and seldom visits them. Your parents seem to be satisfied with things as they are. You would like to get your siblings to shoulder some of the load, but you don't know how to approach them.

Clarify the Problem

1. Does everyone agree a problem exists?

Unfortunately, no one but you (and your husband and children) seem to feel there is a problem.

2. How urgent is the problem, really?

There are no immediate concerns about your parents' health and safety, but you know you can't continue being their sole caregiver indefinitely. You are on the verge of burnout. Therefore, you can't wait too long to find help.

3. What is behind your siblings' problematic behaviors?

At this point, you have no evidence that either sibling will refuse to help if asked. But they have reasons for not offering to become involved. Your sister is too swamped at work to be aware of anyone's needs but her own. She has no incentive to change, either, since your willingness to take care of your parents meets her needs. Your brother may see what you are doing as a woman's responsibility. In addition, since he has never been close to your parents, he is almost certainly more comfortable staying away as much as possible.

4. What's hooking you?

There is no doubt you are concerned about your parents' welfare. However, it is possible you have helped create your own predicament. To find out why, ask yourself how you ended up taking care of your parents in the first place. Are you always the one in the family who attends to everyone else's needs? Do you habitually put your own needs last? It is not unusual for people who behave this way to take on a helping role automatically and then find themselves becoming resentful and depressed when things become overwhelming.

It is also possible that you volunteered because you felt that, as a teacher, your time commitment to your job was not so great as your siblings', who may work longer hours and have less vacation time.

Lastly, you may feel gratified by being the "good" child, more caring than your siblings. Once you begin to play this role, it is hard to break out of it, even when it becomes tiresome.

5. Who must be included in problem-solving discussions?

In addition to your siblings, your parents should be involved. At the very least, you should let them know you need to cut down on the time you spend taking care of them and that you will discuss this with your brother and sister with an eye toward their sharing the responsibilities.

6. What is your goal?

Your goal is to reduce the amount of time you spend taking care of your parents so that you will have more time for yourself and your own family. Ideally, this will be done by persuading your siblings to share the responsibility for your parents' care.

Solve the Problem

1. Decide on the needs your solution must satisfy.

Your solution must provide you with relief from being your parents' only helper. It must also ensure that your parents' current and future needs are satisfied in a way that is acceptable to them. Finally, it must be acceptable to your brother and sister and be practical enough to work for everyone over the long term.

2. Come up with a few possible solutions.

One possibility is for you and your brother and sister to share your parents' shopping and homemaking tasks. How you share them can be decided among the three of you. One of you can do the weekly shopping, another the cleaning, and the third the laundry. Splitting up the tasks will shorten the time any one of you spends helping. Alternately, each of you can assume sole responsibility for all tasks for a week at a time on a rotating basis, thereby ensuring that each of you has at least two weeks to yourself every month.

Another option is to have paid help perform some or all of the tasks. This might suit *both* your sister and brother. There is nothing inherently unacceptable about this, provided the decision is made openly and with appropriate involvement on everyone's part, especially your parents'.

3. Analyze the choices and select the best solution.

GOAL: How can I get relief from being my parents' only helper?

NEEDS	POSSIBLE SOLUTIONS		
	Do nothing	All siblings share responsibility for tasks	Some or all of the tasks are performed by hired help
Must relieve you from being your parents' only helper	no	yes	yes
Must ensure your parents' current needs are met	yes, but you cannot continue doing it all yourself	yes, provided everyone agrees on the arrangements	yes, provided everyone agrees on the arrangements
Must provide for your parents' future needs	no, you are already taking on more than you can cope with	probably, but their future needs will determine this	yes, since the reliance on outsiders can always be increased
Must be acceptable to your parents	yes	probably	uncertain (depends on your parents' willingness to accept outside help)
Must be acceptable to your siblings	yes	uncertain	probably
Must be practical and workable	no	yes, if acceptable to your siblings and carefully planned	probably, provided services are available and affordable

If your siblings are willing to provide hands-on help, then that option is best because it avoids the potential problems associated with hiring outside help.

4. Conduct a Murphy's Law analysis.

If you and your siblings agree to share hands-on care, trouble can arise if either of them fails to hold up his or her part of the bargain. With this in mind, plan for emergencies by arranging a trade-off system—keep track of who does what for whom. However, taking on the responsibility of being the record keeper or assigner of tasks can put you back to square one. To avoid this, share the schedule of allocated responsibilities with your parents. To the extent possible, encourage *them* to speak directly to whichever sibling is responsible for a task that has gone undone. Intervene only if absolutely necessary.

What if your siblings refuse to be involved in any way in your parents' care? It is unusual for family members to refuse to do *anything* at all, especially when provided with options. However, when there is a family history of serious mental illness or strong discord, it happens. (We know of one case in which a family member told a sibling on learning that their mother was seriously ill, "Take Mom to your house and let me know when she dies.") If you reach a total impasse and are unsuccessful using the strategies discussed in chapter 3, it will be up to you to arrange for outside help.

5. Carry out your plan.

Begin by telling your parents of your need to cut back on the amount of time you spend providing care for them, and explain why. Tell them you intend to approach your brother and sister to ask for help. Then call your siblings and explain the situation. You may want to tell them some of the ideas you have been considering and ask them for theirs. Arrange for a family meeting with your siblings and parents to discuss options. (See *Family Meetings* on opposite page.) At the meeting be explicit about why you are having trouble as the sole caregiver. Using *I*-messages (pages 12–13) can be helpful, since they are not blaming or condemning. (If you start accusing your siblings of being uncaring and irresponsible, you won't get very far.)

Family Meetings

For a family meeting to succeed, it is important for everyone to agree on goals and for clear communication guidelines to be set. We suggest the following.

1. Goals

Before the meeting, each person should answer these questions from his or her own perspective:

- What is the problem that makes this meeting necessary?
- Why has our family been unable to solve the problem?
- What do I hope will happen as a result of the meeting—in other words, what will "success" look like?
- What am I willing to do to ensure that the meeting is successful?
- What am I *not* willing to do?

2. Communication guidelines

When emotions run high, it is especially important for rules of behavior to be made clear.

- Family members should speak only for themselves, not for others. (Avoid statements such as, "I'm not the only one upset about this. I know John is upset, too!" and "You all may think I'm crazy but . . .")
- While someone is speaking, no interruptions are allowed. Family members must agree to hear each other out.
- Use *I*-messages (pages 12–13) rather than judging, preaching, blaming, giving advice, or telling others how they need to change for the situation to improve.

continued on next page

Family Meetings—*continued*

- No one should dominate the meeting. If necessary, set time limits.

- Participants should avoid private agreements or secret exchanges. Unless there is a compelling reason (such as protecting a seriously ill parent from information that would be devastating and about which nothing can be done), information should be shared with *all* family members.

If these procedures don't work or if no progress is made after one or two meetings, we recommend enlisting the help of an objective outsider, such as a therapist, to serve as mediator.

Adapted from Joseph A. Ilardo, *As Parents Age: A Psychological and Practical Guide* (Acton, MA: VanderWyk & Burnham, 1998)

Once the problem is clarified, the three of you can decide how to allocate and fulfill the various responsibilities. Throughout the meeting, encourage your siblings to speak with your parents and with each other. Stay out of the middle as much as possible. (If you have reservations about your ability to run this meeting, consider enlisting the help of a family therapist or a person familiar with elder issues to serve as a neutral mediator.)

Once the plan is defined, work out a way for everyone to keep in touch so that adjustments can be made to the plan when necessary. Weekly calls and monthly family meetings might be a good way to do this. Once a caregiving rhythm is set up, these calls and meetings can be made on an as-needed basis.

6. Evaluate your progress

There are many ways to determine how things are going. One is to ask your parents. Another is to use your visits to get a firsthand look. Try to get everyone involved in troubleshooting problems as they arise. Even if your plan is working, you may need to explore other options as your parents' needs change.

~

My mother clearly needs to see a doctor, but she refuses to do so.

Situation

Your 77-year-old mother has been living on her own since your father's death five years ago. Although she never quite recovered emotionally from the loss of her husband, she has been active and self-sufficient. Recently, however, she has complained of feeling tired much of the time. When you visit, you often see her wince in pain and try to stifle her groans. She also smells of urine. Each time you comment on her pain or her groans, or raise the issue of incontinence, she angrily tells you to leave her alone. She has also been losing weight and is clearly not herself.

You have suggested she see a doctor, but she refuses. She blames your father's physician for your father's death, and since that time has had no ongoing relationship with any doctor. A week ago, you and your mother had a stormy exchange about her need to look after her health. When you asked her why she is being so stubborn, she shouted, "I'm in charge of my own life!"

Since your mother is not incompetent, she has the legal right to refuse to see a doctor. However, you suspect she wants help, and because you care about her, you cannot simply turn your back.

Clarify the Problem

1. Does everyone agree a problem exists?

You and your mother both know something is wrong with her. She doesn't dispute that fact. She simply refuses to get help and knows you can't force her to do so.

2. How urgent is the problem, really?

Your mother's distress cannot be taken lightly. Even though the origins of her pain and incontinence may not be serious, they certainly require attention, and the sooner the better.

3. What is behind your mother's problematic behavior?

The treatment your father received prior to his death has led to your mother's distrust of physicians, and she may fear putting herself in their hands. She may also fear what an examination will reveal. In addition, she may be embarrassed to discuss her incontinence.

Although she declares herself "in charge of her life," she is behaving more like a frightened child than a mature, independent woman. Competent adults who take charge of their lives do not typically sacrifice their health or comfort just because they can. Your mother appears to be motivated more by terror than by a desire to run her own life. Unless you want to respect this false independence and walk away, you will have to find some way to get your mother the help she needs, with or without her consent.

4. What's hooking you?

It is upsetting to know that your mother is incontinent and in pain. But your distress may be rooted also in your ambivalence about overriding her clearly stated desires, even though her welfare may be at stake. It is a big step to assume this kind of responsibility and far easier to back down into the role of the good or obedient child.

5. Who must be included in problem-solving discussions?

Although your mother is the one who is ill, she is obviously in no condition to sit down with you and have a rational discussion. You, alone, will have to do your best to see that she gets the help she needs.

6. What is your goal?

The ideal outcome will be for your mother to see a physician right away. However, *any* medical attention, even if provided by a visiting nurse, will be a good start.

Solve the Problem

1. Decide on the needs your solution must satisfy.

Given the potentially serious nature of your mother's condition, the solution must be one that can be implemented without delay. To the extent that it can, your plan should show respect for your mother's need to feel in charge of her life. In addition, the solution should allow her to comply without losing face. Since she has absolutely refused to see a physician up until now, she may feel embarrassed reversing her position, even if she wants to. (You can make it easier for her to do this by letting her know you understand the reasons for her initial refusal.) Finally, the solution must take into account her distrust of physicians. Although convincing her won't be easy, you must address her wariness and reassure her that she can seek a second opinion if she is not comfortable with the first health care provider's diagnosis and treatment plan.

2. Come up with a few possible solutions.

You can try suggesting some alternatives that your mother might find acceptable. For example, if she refuses to see a physician she knows, offer to find her a new one. (Fresh starts sometimes have appeal.) If she refuses to see *any* physician, perhaps she will agree to a visiting nurse. If she remains adamant that she will not see any medical person at this time, ask her to describe conditions under which she *will* accept help. If these conditions are acceptable to you, write them down. Review them with her, and have her promise to abide by them. Given a chance to make the decision, she may be willing to see a physician when *she* feels it is warranted.

You can also tell her about local facilities where she can get help, such as a geriatric health center or a women's health clinic. These more specialized options may be less threatening to her. You can also suggest that you visit them together, just to see what they are like. This may give her a way to change her mind without losing face.

If she is not open to treatment under any conditions, you can enlist the help of relatives, friends, clergy, or anyone else your mother respects and trusts. There is strength in numbers, and your mother may be touched by the sight of so many people expressing concern for her. Together, confront and prevail on her to accept help.

As a last resort, you can report the situation to Adult Protective Services. The task of this agency is to protect elders from abuse, neglect, or exploitation. Your mother's behavior

Adult Protective Services

Every state has an Adult Protective Services Department, sometimes called Protective Services for the Elderly or some equivalent. It is usually one of several departments that comprise the Office of the Aging. Find your state's office by checking your telephone directory's blue pages under "Social Services," "Elder Services," or "Office of the Aging." In the yellow pages look for "Social and Human Services—Elderly Person's Services." Your local Area Agency on Aging can also direct you to the appropriate state office. To locate the nearest AAA, contact the National Association of Area Agencies on Aging at (202) 872-0888 or www.n4a.org/.

would fall under the category of "self-neglect"—sadly, a common occurrence. A caseworker would investigate her situation and make a recommendation based on the facts. Immediate action might or might not follow, depending on the caseworker's assessment. However, even if immediate action were not taken, the threat that the state could take control might be enough to convince your mother to act on her own behalf.

3. Analyze the choices and select the best solution.

GOAL: How can I get my mother medical help?

	POSSIBLE SOLUTIONS			
NEEDS	Do nothing	Propose alternatives to seeing a physician she already knows	Enlist help to convince her to get medical attention	Call in Adult Protective Services
Must be able to be implemented quickly	n/a	yes	yes	yes
Must respect your mother's need to feel in control of her life	yes, but this is not in her best interest	yes	yes	no
Must enable your mother to accept help without losing face	n/a	yes, if handled sensitively	yes, if planned carefully	no
Must take into account her distrust of physicians	yes, but this is not in her best interest	yes	yes, if planned carefully	no

The preferred solution is to suggest some alternatives that your mother might find acceptable.

4. Conduct a Murphy's Law analysis.

If your mother rejects all your alternative suggestions, you can try asking people your mother respects to participate in an orchestrated confrontation, during which everyone will try to convince your mother to accept help. Discuss your goal with them, set a date, and tell your mother about the meeting. Be prepared to act as a moderator during the course of the meeting. If your mother finally agrees to accept help, be ready to act quickly, before she changes her mind again. That might mean literally being prepared to take her to a doctor's office or other facility *that day*.

Your mother may also shut down completely and, regardless of how you approach her, refuse to talk about anything pertinent to her care. At this point, all you can do is stay calm. Do not allow your frustration to turn to anger. Instead, tell her in a very matter-of-fact way that you are sorry she is treating herself so badly and that you will have to see to it that she gets the help she needs. Although she is sure to give you a hard time, she may actually be relieved to have the decision taken out of her hands.

5. Carry out your plan.

Before speaking with your mother, do your homework. Through your own doctor, or through relatives, friends, or local senior centers, generate a list of a few physicians who are sensitive to the needs of elderly people. Speak with them, explain the situation, and use their responses to gauge their competence and caring, as well as the likelihood of their being acceptable to your mother. Keep searching until you find at least two doctors who impress you favorably and who seem likely to win your mother's approval. Record their names, addresses, and phone numbers, along with your personal impressions, so that you can refer to these notes later. When you speak with your mother, share your reactions to these doctors. Make a case in favor of one in particular, and do your best to convince her to give him or her a try. You will need all the persuasive arguments you can muster to convince her to agree.

Similarly, contact a visiting nurse or other home health service and preselect several experienced nurse practitioners who can be called on in case your mother agrees to that option. Locate and visit any specialized health centers that might meet your mother's needs. Record the names and phone numbers of the people you meet who might be able to help.

When speaking with your mother, you must remember to support her desire to be in charge. Let her know that you see your role as helping her, not as taking over. You can do this by allowing her to be the one to choose among the options you have provided, and by allowing her to do this at her own pace.

6. Evaluate your progress.

You will know you have succeeded when your mother agrees to accept medical care. If she continues to refuse or she postpones action to some indefinite time in the future, you will have no choice but to exert more pressure and, if necessary, call Adult Protective Services.

֍

My mother is not poor,
but she skimps to save money.

Situation

Your widowed mother, 88, is a retired physician. She is financially well-off because she managed her investments wisely over the years. A few years ago she sold her home and moved into a nicely furnished, air-conditioned condominium. She maintains an active social calendar for a woman her age. She serves on the boards of her local library and senior center, reads widely, and generally enjoys herself.

Although you and your two sisters are delighted with the life your mother has made for herself, there is one thing she has been doing for the last several months—something out of character for her—that drives you all crazy. Your mother insists on skimping on day-to-day expenses. Sometimes she travels long distances to certain stores where she knows she can save a few dollars off toiletries and cosmetics. When she shops for food, she buys cold-cut ends and cuts of meat that are "manager's specials"—almost, but not quite, out-of-date. She also buys cans of food that are dented and therefore sold at reduced prices. At home, she fiddles with her thermostat, lowering it in the winter to save on heating oil and raising it in the summer to save on air-conditioning costs. As a result, almost every time you visit her, you find her home insufferably warm or cold. (She claims she is perfectly comfortable and boasts about the money she saves.) Although you are unaware of her having become ill as a result of her scrimping, it is a constant source of worry.

You and your sisters are puzzled and dismayed by her behavior and have spoken with her about it. You have admonished her gently about her unnecessary frugality. "Mom, you have more than enough money in the bank and in your mutual funds. You don't need to live like this!" Your words so far have been wasted. She insists she is living exactly as she wishes and says there is no harm in her shopping for bargains. "I know what I'm doing," she has said more than once, and she has made it clear that your gentle reminders are not welcome.

Clarify the Problem

1. Does everyone agree a problem exists?

Your mother is completely comfortable with her frugal lifestyle. Moreover, there is no evidence that her behavior is causing her to suffer in any way. Consequently, it is premature to say that there is—objectively speaking—an actual problem. Still, the fact that this behavior is uncharacteristic of her concerns you. So the only "problem" at the moment is that you and your sisters are upset.

2. How urgent is the problem, really?

Nothing about the situation is urgent. However, two factors represent legitimate worries. First, your mother could make an error in judgment and buy something that really makes her sick. Second, this change in behavior is relatively recent and may indicate that something is amiss and should not be ignored.

3. What is behind your mother's problematic behavior?

Whenever anyone begins behaving in ways that are out of character or different from the usual, it is always appropriate to investigate. What you find out may be trivial, or it may be significant.

With your mother, for example, it may be that her social

calendar is not as active as you thought; she could be motivated by loneliness and be using bargain hunting to fill her empty days. Or it may be that she simply enjoys saving money, and shopping for bargains allows her to use her still-sharp mind to find good values. She may also be trying to save money to be sure she is never really impoverished or to maximize the size of the estate she will leave to you and your sisters. Furthermore, she may truly be comfortable keeping the temperature at the levels she chooses. Just because you are too cold or too warm does not mean that she is.

A more troubling explanation is that these changes are early signs of an underlying problem with her emotions or thinking. If, over time, your mother experiences unexplained bouts of anger or depression, or forgets how to do things she has always done with ease, it is advisable to have her evaluated by her personal physician as soon as possible.

4. What's hooking you?

In addition to your concern for your mother's health, you may feel embarrassed by her engaging in this uncharacteristic behavior, worried that others will fault you for allowing her to live as though she were poor.

5. Who must be included in problem-solving discussions?

At this point, there is no need for a formal, problem-solving discussion. However, if your mother becomes ill as a result of her scrimping or begins to act strangely, then you and your sisters will certainly want to take a stronger stand with her about what is happening.

6. What is your goal?

Your goal is preventive in nature. You want to convince your mother to stop skimping and to live in a style consistent with her financial resources. That means shopping at local stores, buying fresh, wholesome foods, and keeping her thermostat at a constant, comfortable temperature.

Solve the Problem

1. Decide on the needs your solution must satisfy.

Whatever you do, you *must* respect your mother's right to live as she wants, whether you like it or not. There are only two conditions under which you can legitimately override her preferences: (1) if she becomes ill as a result of her actions, or (2) if she exhibits unsafe behaviors due to mental incompetence.

Your solution must also allow you and your sisters to feel that you are doing all you can for your mother.

Finally, the solution must give you the opportunity to speak with your mother about what she is doing, so that you can better understand her motivations as well as observe whether additional changes in her behavior warrant an examination by her physician.

2. Come up with a few possible solutions.

While doing nothing is rarely the best way to resolve dilemmas with elderly parents, sometimes a wait-and-see approach makes sense. In this case it may, though you might want to discuss your decision with your mother, explaining that you won't interfere with her life as long as she seems to be doing well. However, if her skimping puts her at risk, you will want to step in.

You may also choose to speak with your mother from time to time to understand her motivations and to remind her that she need not skimp because of any financial need.

Another option that might set your mind at ease is to take over your mother's shopping.

3. Analyze the choices and select the best solution.

(See chart on next page.)

The best solution is to check in with your mother periodically to see how she is doing. This will satisfy you that you are doing something, without going so far as to undermine your mother's autonomy.

GOAL: How can I persuade my mother to stop skimping?

	POSSIBLE SOLUTIONS		
NEEDS	Do nothing (but wait and see)	Keep in touch to understand motivations, to evaluate behavior, and to remind of financial situation	Take over the shopping
Must respect your mother's right to live as she wants	yes	yes	no
Must ensure your mother's health and safety	yes, unless you fail to act when something changes	yes	yes
Must satisfy you and your sisters that you are doing what you can for your mother	no	as much as is possible, short of taking control of her life	yes
Must enable you and your sisters to observe your mother for signs of a problem for which your mother might need to be examined	yes	yes	possibly, but your taking control may hide the problem

4. Conduct a Murphy's Law analysis.

Since your solution asks little of your mother, it is unlikely much can go wrong. There is, however, no guarantee that she will speak with you about her behavior, especially if you badger her with your concerns. Should she shut down, you will need to apologize and back off, bearing in mind the important principle that if she chooses to skimp, that is her right, as long as she remains healthy.

5. Carry out your plan.

Your plan has three aspects. The first is to observe your mother during the time you spend with her. If you feel that she is thinking or acting in decidedly strange ways, a thorough evaluation by her physician is advisable. Convincing her to undergo this exam will become the actual problem you need to solve.

The second aspect is to be sure she has an accurate view of her financial resources. Every so often, you might ask respectfully to review her bank statements and mutual fund updates with you. This will serve to remind her of the money she has available. As a result, she might reconsider her behavior. Or, if appropriate, you might ask her financial advisor or the family lawyer to speak with her periodically, as a way to remind her of her assets.

The third aspect is to let her know how her lifestyle choices affect you and your sisters. While respecting her right to live as she wishes, you will nevertheless be conveying your distress that she is not living as well or as comfortably as she can.

6. Evaluate your progress.

One indication of success is that your mother stops skimping. If you notice that she is shopping in more convenient, local stores and bringing better-quality foods into her home, and if you observe that the temperature is more comfortable when you visit, you will know that your words and strategies made a difference.

Another indication of success is that your mother may not change her behavior at all but you and your sisters feel satisfied that she is fine and is choosing this lifestyle for reasons you can accept.

ॐ

My sisters argue constantly about taking care of our parents, and everyone calls *me* for help.

Situation

You have two sisters, Jane and Samantha, who are both married and have college-age children. They live near your parents, who are in their early 80s. You moved away from the area several years ago, when your spouse changed jobs. You miss your family and wish you could see them more often.

Six months ago your parents were involved in an auto accident. Your mother broke her leg, and your father suffered a concussion and a broken hip. Your sisters stepped in immediately to take care of your parents and worked out ways to share responsibility for their care. Since the accident, you visit once a month, keep in touch by phone, and try to be supportive of all of them. Although your parents are getting better, neither has recovered as quickly as expected. As a result, your sisters have found themselves doing a great deal more than they had imagined and for a much longer period of time.

Lately, things have begun to deteriorate. Your sisters are arguing about many things. For example, Samantha feels Jane isn't sharing enough of the responsibilities. Jane feels Samantha is a control freak, who won't allow her to have a say in decisions.

Each sister calls you to complain about the other. Even more upsetting to you, though, is that now your parents are calling you as well, very distressed by the conflict between your sisters. Last night your mother cried, "I can't take this any more. Your father and I are too much of a burden on them. Maybe we should go live in a nursing home."

Clarify the Problem

1. Does everyone agree a problem exists?

There is no denying on anyone's part that a problem exists. The tension that has developed between your sisters is affecting your sisters' relationship and your parents' peace of mind. You are unhappy being in the middle.

2. How urgent is the problem, really?

This problem is fairly urgent. The level of distress is high for everyone and could possibly result in your sisters' providing inadequate care for your parents. Although your parents are much better off in their own home, their guilt may lead them to insist on institutionalized care. At that point, if your sisters see no end to their conflict, they may agree with your parents. You live too far away to offer hands-on support, but you *are* in a position to help everyone see what is happening and to propose some alternatives.

3. What is behind your sisters' problematic behaviors?

Some of the reasons for your sisters' discord are obvious. Since your parents' recovery has been slower than expected, your sisters have become long-term caregivers, with no end in sight, instead of short-term caregivers. Thrown into this role abruptly, they probably did not anticipate the impact of their decision on their own lives and families.

It is not clear, however, why your sisters are unable to work out their disagreements now. It is possible that some past rivalries over who is the "better" child are being played out. Or they may resent your not sharing the load and may be trying to draw you into the situation with their complaints. However, since your sisters got along well initially, it is probable that their increased tension and distress are the result of the pressures of caregiving and are warning signs of burnout.

4. What's hooking you?

You are legitimately upset about your parents' and sisters' predicament and probably feel guilty about living so far away. In addition, your family has come at you from all sides, expecting that you will somehow make things better. You would be superhuman if you *didn't* feel tremendous stress under these circumstances.

That stress can hurt you in two ways. First, it may tempt you to try to solve the problem quickly and single-handedly without making use of available resources. Second, it may prevent you from acknowledging—let alone expressing—the anger and resentment you almost certainly feel at being cast in the role of family savior. These buried feelings may erupt unexpectedly in the form of impatience or annoyance with your parents or sisters, thereby undermining your efforts to help.

5. Who must be included in problem-solving discussions?

Everyone should be involved, but not all at once. You will need to talk with your sisters to discuss their complaints and difficulties. You will also need to talk with your parents, if only to reassure them that the family can work out these problems.

6. What is your goal?

Your goal is to find a way for your parents to receive adequate care at home without putting undue stress on your sisters or yourself.

Solve the Problem

1. Decide on the needs your solution must satisfy.

Obviously your solution must ensure that your parents' physical needs are met without their feeling that they are a burden. Your sisters need relief from some of their caregiving obligations and to have time for their own lives. You also want the frequency of distress calls from your sisters and parents reduced. Finally, your solution must preserve the family's financial resources.

2. Come up with a few possible solutions.

A few options exist. The first is to help your sisters work out their conflicts so they can continue caring for your parents by themselves. A second option is to have your parents receive care from some combination of your sisters and hired professionals. The number of hours per week and services provided will have to be negotiated with costs in mind. A third option is to have professionals provide all the care until your parents can manage on their own. Again, finances will have to be taken into account. Finally, your parents can go to a rehabilitation or assisted living facility if there is an appropriate and affordable one nearby. (There is a caution here: Your mother's stated desire to go into a home appeared to be motivated primarily by guilt and distress and is probably not an indication of her true feelings. Therefore, knowing your parents' preferences and considering their emotional needs is particularly important.)

3. Analyze the choices and select the best solution.

(See chart on next page.)

The best option for everyone at this time is to arrange for part-time home care to help your sisters take care of your parents.

4. Conduct a Murphy's Law analysis.

Despite your best efforts, you may be unable to help your sisters resolve their conflicts to the degree that they can work together, even with the help of paid home care. If this happens, enlisting

GOAL: How can my parents get adequate care without demanding too much of my sisters or myself?

	POSSIBLE SOLUTIONS				
NEEDS	Do nothing	Help your sisters resolve their conflicts so they can continue providing care	Arrange for some of the home care to be done by professionals	Arrange for all of the home care to be done by professionals	Place your parents in a rehabilitation or assisted living facility
Must meet your parents' physical and emotional needs	yes, but not for long	yes	yes	physical needs, yes; emotional needs, unlikely	physical needs, yes; emotional needs, unlikely
Must give your sisters relief from some of the caregiving	no	no	yes	yes	yes
Must reduce the frequency of distress calls you receive	no	yes	probably	yes	most likely
Must preserve family financial resources	yes	yes	possibly	no	no

the help of an objective party such as a mental health worker may be advisable.

Even if your sisters resolve their conflicts and agree on a home care plan, its success is not certain. First of all, it may be difficult to find or pay for outside resources, in which case the entire family may need to discuss options and expenses with local professionals such as social workers, or with staff members in your state's Office of the Aging.

There may be a delay while a suitable agency and skilled people are found. Once that is accomplished, there will almost certainly be an adjustment period while both your parents and sisters get used to the new arrangement. Issues of territoriality often emerge when outsiders enter a home to provide care. This adjustment period requires patience on everyone's part. Your sisters will also have to learn to work closely with the home care workers to decide who will be responsible for what.

It is also possible that the aides you select do not work out. Lack of experience, training, or skill may make them inappropriate, or your sisters or parents may not like them. In that case, you will need to start over to find more suitable help. (See *Choosing a Home Health Agency* on next page.)

5. Carry out your plan.

Since you have already been delegated the peacemaker, you can use this to your advantage to implement your plan. The following steps make sense:

- Before doing anything, tell your sisters that you need to meet with them to clarify what their complaints and difficulties are and to generate possible solutions. (The principles of communication discussed in chapter 2 will guide you in your discussion.)

- Before meeting with your sisters, tell your parents what you are planning, and promise to report back to them after you and your sisters talk. Reassure them that there are many options available, short of "putting them away," and that their input will be needed and valued.

- Meet with your sisters at a mutually convenient place. Since your sisters live near each other, you will probably have to travel. This means, in turn, that you will want to discuss your intentions with your spouse, children, and employer—anyone who may be affected by your absence—and make plans to minimize its impact.

- Finally, during your meeting with your sisters, encourage them to talk about their specific dissatisfactions and to find ways to get beyond their differences. Even if they are successful, your sisters might want to consider seeking the ongoing support of

Choosing a Home Health Agency

Home health agencies are listed in the telephone directory's yellow pages under "Home Health Services." For recommendations, ask your parents' physicians, the director of the social work department at their local hospital, and the directors of local senior centers or adult day-care facilities.

For more general information, check the telephone directory's blue pages for the county's Social Services Department or Office of the Aging, or check the yellow pages under "Social Services—Elderly Person's Services." Another excellent source of information is the local Area Agency on Aging. To locate the nearest AAA, call the National Association of Area Agencies on Aging at (202) 872-0888 or visit their Web site at www.n4a.org/.

Once you have located a few home health agencies, screen each one for quality by applying the following criteria.

Find out about licensing and certification.

• Is the agency Medicare certified?

• Is it licensed by the state? (Not all states require licensing. Check with the state's Office of the Aging.)

• Is it accredited by the Joint Commission of Accreditation of Health Care Organizations?

Find out about policies that govern their operation.

• Does the agency provide coverage 24 hours a day, 7 days a week?

• Is a home visit arranged prior to taking on a client, and periodically thereafter, to monitor care?

• What are the hiring policies? Are general and/or criminal background checks performed? Are references checked? Are personal interviews conducted?

Choosing a Home Health Agency—*continued*

- Are the agency's caregivers licensed or certified? By whom? Are they insured and bonded?

- Will the same caregiver be providing help to the extent possible, or will caregivers change? What happens if a caregiver is unable to come to work? (Don't hesitate to ask whether the caregiver has reliable transportation.)

Find out about the services provided.

- What services are available through the agency?

- How long is the waiting period between the time services are requested and the time services begin?

Find out about costs, payment policies, and insurance.

- How are fees calculated? Are there any up-front costs?

- Will your parents be expected to pay the caregiver directly, or will they pay the agency?

- What are eligibility requirements for care recipients? What documents are required to verify eligibility?

- Does the agency accept assignment? (This means that the agency will agree to limit charges to the amounts approved by an insurer such as Medicare. In such cases, the agency bills the insurer directly for services. The insurer pays a set percentage of approved charges; the beneficiary pays the balance. There is almost always an annual deductible that must first be met. Since insurance rules are constantly in flux, verify the exact arrangements with the agency.)

- Will the agency provide services if the insurance expires?

a professional. This can help them deal with the effects that their extended caregiving is having on themselves and on their families.

Your family also will need to explore the services available in your parents' community and compare the costs. All of you will need to select an agency, arrange for the appropriate aides, and work out allocation of responsibilities. Make sure your sisters and parents are comfortable with the agency and the people selected. If they are not, the plan cannot succeed.

6. Evaluate your progress.

You will know whether your plan is succeeding by the feedback you receive from your parents and sisters. This means that your parents and sisters all say they are satisfied, and the frantic phone calls stop. On the other hand, if your sisters continue to call and your parents remain distressed, you will know that some aspect of your plan is failing and needs to be reevaluated.

My 82-year-old father wants to marry a woman he just met.

Situation

Your well-to-do father has been a widower for nearly a decade. He had difficulty adjusting to your mother's death but has come to terms with it over time. During the past few years he has been active and seems happy. He regularly attends meetings at his senior center and is popular there because of his pleasing manner, worldliness, and inherent charm. Furthermore, at 82, he still drives. It's little wonder that he is "in demand" among the women at the center, a fact that has long pleased and amused you. You and your brother have always had a good relationship with him, and he has made it clear that you and your families will be well taken care of after his death.

Two weeks ago your father telephoned early on a Saturday morning, an unusual time for him, and asked whether he might come by to speak with you as soon as it was convenient. You arranged to meet him at a local restaurant for breakfast. During your visit he told you that he had met a woman recently and had fallen in love. "Sandy is 62, and she's only been widowed for a year," he said. "The two of us have never been happier." Then he broke the real news—they planned to marry in six weeks. You were speechless. The rest of the conversation was a blur. All you could think was, I've got to get home and call Andy. Your hope was that your brother and you, with the help of your spouses, could talk some sense into your father.

Three days after the conversation in the restaurant, the four of you made an attempt to talk to your father over dinner at your home. It was a disaster. He was eager to share his good news with all of you and didn't seem to notice the looks of concern behind the frozen smiles on your faces. You and Andy, struggling to find the right words, told him how shocked and worried you were about his decision to get married to a woman he just met. He seemed hurt at first, but then he became angry. Try as you might to smooth things over, your true feelings were clear, and he was deeply offended. He retained his composure but left the table early, explaining that he needed to get home. The four of you felt awful. Since that time, each of you has called him, but your messages have gone unanswered.

Clarify the Problem

1. Does everyone agree a problem exists?

You, your brother, and your spouses feel there is a problem, but it is clear your father doesn't. You are disturbed by the speed with which he has made his decision and the potential impact on him and the rest of the family. You worry about the hurt he may suffer should the relationship not work out. Moreover, given the 20-year difference in their ages, you are concerned that Sandy's interest is primarily in your father's money.

The only problem as far as your father is concerned is that his family is displeased at the prospect of something that is, to him, a source of tremendous joy.

2. How urgent is the problem, really?

The proposed wedding date is only a few weeks away. If you had any doubt about your father's determination, your unreturned phone calls should dispel that. He *will* marry Sandy if something isn't done soon to get him to change his mind.

3. What is behind your father's problematic behavior?

Your father's falling in love is no more explainable than anyone else's. However, the fact that he refuses to talk about his decision to marry suggests that he may not want to look too closely at the issues that trouble you and your brother. His hurt and anger at your reactions are genuine, but so is his denial of the complexities of his decision.

4. What's hooking you?

You worry about your father. Although his mind appears to be clear and his judgment sound, you can't help seeing the potential for emotional disaster for him and financial disaster for the entire family.

5. Who must be included in problem-solving discussions?

Your father, your brother, and you must be involved in discussions about your father's decision.

6. What is your goal?

You have neither the right nor the power to stop your father from marrying. You cannot have him declared incompetent, because he isn't. Nor can you treat him like a love-sick teenager and ship him off to some faraway place. Your goal, therefore, is twofold. First, you must find a way to satisfy yourself that Sandy genuinely cares about him, and second, you must make sure that even after your father marries, his estate is protected.

To accomplish your goal, you need to convince your father to slow down and wait a little longer before getting married. This will allow you and your family time to get to know Sandy and will give your father time to consider what he wants to do about his estate. (A prenuptial agreement is most likely the simplest protection. However, prenuptial agreements were uncommon when your father and mother married, and he might not have thought to use one now. Also, it is likely that when he first married, there was no estate to protect.)

Solve the Problem

1. Decide on the needs your solution must satisfy.

Your solution must show your father that you and your brother value his happiness and that you are not trying to run his life. It must give you a chance to get to know Sandy to determine whether there is any cause for alarm. Regardless of Sandy's motives, however, your solution must guarantee that your father's estate is protected. Finally, if necessary, it must allow your father to change his mind without losing face.

2. Come up with a few possible solutions.

You and your brother haven't had much chance to share your concerns with your father, so one option is to arrange another meeting with him to talk things over with open minds. Two aspects of such a meeting deserve attention—your father's emotional well-being and his finances. You will seem uncaring if, after being out of touch, you arrange a meeting solely to discuss his plans for your inheritance. So a first step will be to talk with him more about his plans and his relationship with Sandy.

You may consider trying immediately to convince your father to delay his wedding date so that you and your family can talk with him about how his plans may affect all of you. This is especially important if you are afraid that one of his reasons for rushing into the marriage is that he would rather not look at the very issues that are concerning you.

Another option is to invite your father to bring Sandy for a visit to introduce her to the family. Getting to know her and seeing how she interacts with him may lead later to a candid discussion of your father's financial plans. You and your brother, your spouses, your father, and Sandy should participate in that discussion. Including everyone will prevent misunderstandings and will give you a chance to see where Sandy stands on this issue.

3. Analyze the choices and select the best solution.

GOAL: How can I ensure that my father's marriage won't jeopardize his well-being or his estate?

	POSSIBLE SOLUTIONS				
NEEDS	Do nothing	Speak with your father about his plans and share your concerns	Convince your father to delay his marriage in order to explore its implications	Invite your father to bring Sandy to a family gathering, so everyone can get to know her	Have a candid discussion about your father's financial plans
Must satisfy your father that you and your brother are not trying to run his life	yes	possibly	yes, if the reasons for wanting the delay are understood and accepted	yes	yes, if your father agrees that this discussion is necessary
Must give you a chance to evaluate Sandy's motives	no	no, unless your father says something about this	no, but it will allow you time to do so	yes, since you will see her interacting with your father	yes, since her reaction will probably reveal her motives
Must guarantee the family's interest in his estate is protected	no	no, since the purpose of the conversation is simply to get information	no, but it will allow you time to discuss the implications	no	possibly, depending on the outcome of the discussion
Must allow your father to change his mind without losing face	n/a	yes, if he agrees with your concerns	yes, since it gives him time to think about what he is planning to do	yes, if her behavior reveals dubious motives	yes, since if Sandy gives your father a hard time, it will be apparent what her motives are

The preferred solution is a combination of the proposed actions. Since you don't know what financial or legal arrangements your father has already made or what Sandy's motives are, you will have to base your action plan on what you find out once you start talking.

4. Conduct a Murphy's Law analysis.

If your father is sufficiently upset, he may continue to refuse to speak with you and your brother. In that case, an apology and explanation of why you are concerned may convince him to resume contact.

If he refuses to take any steps to protect your inheritance or accuses you of being interested only in his money, you might prevail on his attorney or financial advisor to discuss with him the implications of the situation. They or some neutral party, such as a trusted friend, may be able to help change his mind.

5. Carry out your plan.

Your first step is to reestablish contact with your father. This may not be easy since he has not been returning your calls. If you can't convince him to call you back, try another approach, such as visiting him at a time he is likely to be home.

Just as important as reconnecting with him is knowing what you will say when you do. Think of what he is likely to be feeling. You threw cold water on his surprise; as a result he came away feeling hurt. He is probably expecting more of the same. Make it clear immediately that this is not what you are there for. Instead, let him know you understand his distress. "Dad," you might say, "I know you're very upset, and I don't blame you. You expected Andy and me to be happy for you, and we let you down. We were shocked, and we're worried." Remarks like this can let him know you understand his reactions, while making it clear that your responses were due to your own surprise and distress.

Expect to spend some time getting your relationship on sound footing again. Once you do, you can be more specific about your concerns. If all goes well, you may be able to persuade him to delay his marriage until all of you have had a chance to meet Sandy, to talk things over, and to ensure that his finances are in order. (If he refuses to postpone his wedding, you will have to work quickly to find out what you need to know.)

The resolution of this dilemma involves many steps. Meeting Sandy and gauging her motives as well as making a judgment about the soundness of their relationship are essential. This must be accomplished in a nonthreatening way, in the context of casual family gatherings, not formal discussions or interrogations. Once again, strategic planning and preparation are important. You do not want to give your father and Sandy the impression that they must justify their relationship or their plans. Nor is it wise to place Sandy on trial, as though she were up to no good. (The possibility exists, after all, that she may have more money than your father and that her family sees *him* as the gold digger!) At the same time, you must satisfy yourselves that nothing is seriously amiss.

As a result of these family conversations, your hesitation about your father's plans may disappear. It may become apparent that he and Sandy have been open and thoughtful in their plans and that there are no extraordinary emotional or financial risks bound up with the proposed marriage. In that case, you can support their plans enthusiastically.

However, if you come away convinced that Sandy is out for herself, you owe it to your father and yourself to share your doubts. This may be difficult because your reservations are not something your father wants to hear. Even if Sandy reveals that her motives are less than pure, your father may still refuse to see it. (After all, he would lose face if it became clear that he had misjudged her.) At that point all you can do is try to persuade him, using her own words and other facts to bolster your case.

On the other hand, he may surprise you and reveal that he secretly harbored the same concerns. (That may explain his refusal to hear you out in the first place.) Having seen Sandy's negative reactions to his intention to protect his estate, he may muster the courage to acknowledge his error. Should this be the case, you would be in the ironic position of having established what you hoped wasn't true, making it both fortunate and unfortunate that you succeeded.

6. Evaluate your progress.

You will know that you are on the right track if your father is willing to talk openly with you and your brother. What happens next depends on the soundness of his plans. If he and Sandy are well matched and willing to protect the family estate, and if they have done so already, you need go no further. But suppose your father has failed to make such plans. In that case, you will know you are succeeding when he is willing to take the time to do so and is open about this with Sandy.

If Sandy's interest in your father is primarily financial, family discussions will soon uncover that. It will be difficult for Sandy *not* to reveal her hand as she sees her free ride slipping away. If this happens, the best you can hope for is that your father sees through her and wisely ends the relationship, in which case you can give him whatever support is necessary. If Sandy turns out to be self-serving, but your father remains adamant, even resisting the advice of neutral parties, your only option is to back off, warn your father that you think he is making a terrible mistake, tell him you love him, and then let him do what he wants. Hopefully, removing the pressure for him to do what *you* want will allow him to change his mind.

॰꒰

My mother is doing fine, but she won't listen to her doctor's advice.

Situation

Your 90-year-old mother is in very good health, and her physician describes her as an "amazing woman." Agile, intellectually sharp, and independent, she lives in her small home with the help of an aide who comes in three days a week to take her shopping and help with homemaking tasks. Your mother describes herself as stubborn, and although she has a pleasant relationship with her physician, the two of them rarely see eye to eye when it comes to her care. She sees him when it suits her, which is not as often as he would like, and she cancels routine appointments if she is feeling well. She also ignores many of his recommendations.

Last week you took your mother for her annual physical. As you sat in the waiting room, you mentioned to her that the doctor would probably recommend testing and other procedures as part of a complete medical workup. Her response, said with a smile, was, "The answer is 'no,' no matter what he says."

During the meeting, the doctor recommended typical procedures, such as a Pap smear, a mammogram, and a tetanus shot. To these suggestions she responded, "Leave me alone, doctor. I'm doing fine"; "Let me be, doctor; I'm 90 years old. I can't live forever"; and "Please leave me alone. I've got no pains, no aches."

(In each case, the doctor respectfully acquiesced.) To your surprise, however, she agreed to other recommendations, such as taking a thyroid function test, since she has been feeling tired and chilly more often than usual.

While the doctor does not insist on your mother's total compliance, he is concerned about her refusing tests and procedures he feels are warranted. He has spoken with you privately and has indicated he may not continue to see her if she insists on rejecting his advice.

Clarify the Problem

1. Does everyone agree a problem exists?

The three people involved vary in their concerns. You are worried that your mother's habit of picking and choosing among her doctor's recommendations is not providing her with appropriate overall care. Your mother sees no problem with this at all. And the doctor is ambivalent about the situation. On the one hand, he admires your mother's spirit and recognizes her good health. On the other hand, he is concerned about fulfilling his responsibilities to her and the possibility of leaving himself vulnerable to a malpractice suit. Nevertheless, he is not so distressed as to tell your mother directly that he can no longer see her under these circumstances.

2. How urgent is the problem, really?

This problem is not an urgent one since your mother is currently well. However, her tendency to reject recommended procedures unless they make sense to her may have negative consequences down the road. Her refusal could result in a failure to be diagnosed with a serious but treatable condition in a timely manner.

3. What is behind your mother's problematic behavior?

By her own admission, your mother is a willful person. She knows exactly what she wants and does not want. She has a strong sense of herself and her position as a woman who has lived to be 90 years old.

In addition, although your mother lacks medical knowledge, she is mentally competent and entirely capable of selecting which medical procedures she feels she needs. In fact, she does have a common sense–based rationale for her decisions—she speaks with friends in her seniors group. As a result of what they have learned from their own experiences and from those of others, her friends appear to have agreed tacitly on a set of guidelines for making choices among procedures doctors recommend. (On the way back from the doctor's office last week, your mother explained why she had refused a Pap smear, citing women who were worse off after they allowed others to begin "poking and prodding them.")

It is also likely that fear contributes to your mother's behavior. At her age, she may be afraid to know what is happening inside her body. Furthermore, even if something was uncovered, she would probably elect to forego treatment. Her fatalistic thinking is summarized in her statement, "I can't live forever."

4. What's hooking you?

You are understandably concerned about your mother's well-being. However, less obvious factors may also be at work. For example, you may feel that the doctor will think you are irresponsible for not urging your mother to go along with what he wants. You are caught squarely in the middle, trying to satisfy both your mother's and the doctor's wishes at the same time.

You also know you will feel terrible if you allow your mother to skip a recommended appointment or procedure and then a health problem becomes evident later. For instance, suppose a Pap smear could catch a malignancy that is easily treated?

Moreover, you have mixed feelings about the doctor's acquiescence to your mother's wishes. Although you are pleased with his respect and caring, you are concerned that his failure to take a stronger stand—perhaps insisting that she agree to recommended procedures and keep scheduled appointments—will actually lead to his eventual refusal to treat her.

5. Who must be included in problem-solving discussions?

The people involved are primarily your mother and her physician, and secondarily you.

6. What is your goal?

Your goal is to have your mother and her physician arrive at a workable compromise regarding her medical care—probably fewer procedures and appointments than he wants and more than she thinks are necessary.

Solve the Problem

1. Decide on the needs your solution must satisfy.

Your solution must satisfy your mother's need to feel in control of her medical treatment. It must also satisfy the doctor that he is providing responsible treatment. You also must feel satisfied that you have done all you can to ensure that your mother is getting the medical care she needs.

2. Come up with a few possible solutions.

One solution is for you to encourage your mother to work things out with her doctor so that they both are satisfied with her care plan. If they can't do this, you can intervene and offer to serve as a mediator to help them come to an agreement. As a last resort, if your mother and her physician cannot reach any sort of compromise, you will have to help your mother find another doctor.

3. Analyze the choices and select the best solution.

(See chart on opposite page.)

The best solution is to encourage your mother and her doctor to resolve their differences without your intervention. This is one

GOAL: How can my mother and her doctor agree on my mother's care?

NEEDS	POSSIBLE SOLUTIONS			
	Do nothing	Encourage your mother to work things out with her doctor	Help your mother and her doctor reach a compromise	Help your mother find another doctor
Must satisfy your mother's desire to maintain control of her treatment	yes	yes	probably	yes, but the same problem may occur
Must satisfy the doctor's need to provide responsible treatment	no	possibly	possibly	no
Must satisfy you that you have done all you can to ensure your mother is getting the medical care she needs	no	yes, if they are successful	probably	possibly, depending on how successful you are

of those instances in which it is optimal to initiate a process and then remain on the sidelines, in case you are needed.

4. Conduct a Murphy's Law analysis.

You may need to help your mother and her physician work out their differences after all. For example, you may need to meet with them together to help clarify points of contention and to suggest compromises. If your intervention still fails to break the deadlock and their relationship reaches an impasse, you can help ease the transition to another doctor by asking for referrals and arranging for the transfer of her records.

5. Carry out your plan.

Begin by telling your mother that her doctor has told you he may not be willing to continue treating her unless she and he can come to an agreement about her care. Explain that when she cancels appointments and refuses to follow his recommendations, this upsets him. Let her know he is reluctant to continue assuming responsibility for her medical care unless she is willing to take his advice. Remind your mother she likes this doctor, and ask her whether she is willing to speak with him about their differences. If she agrees, call the doctor. Tell him you have encouraged your mother to talk to him, and ask whether he is willing to speak with her. If he is—and it seems likely since he admires her—set up an appointment.

Before the meeting, ask your mother whether she would like help preparing what she wants to say to the doctor. If she does, work with her on a plan. Let her know it will be important for her to explain her reasoning to the doctor so that he understands her motives. At the same time, be sure she realizes that the doctor will likewise present his reasons for having recommended the various procedures over which they disagreed.

Ask your mother whether she would like you to attend the meeting or if she prefers to do this on her own. If you attend the meeting, try to talk as little as you can. The more your mother is able to clarify by herself, the more satisfied she will feel, and the more likely she will honor whatever agreement is reached. Intervene more actively only if the two of them come to a standstill and are unable to work out their disagreements.

6. Evaluate your progress.

You will know the dilemma has been resolved successfully if your mother and her doctor are no longer at odds about her care. Increased compliance and the absence of complaints on your mother's part, along with reduced concern on the doctor's part, will be reliable measures of success.

~

My husband resents
my father's demands on me.

Situation

Your 73-year-old father has never really been self-sufficient. As the youngest child in his family, he was never asked to do much for himself, and he came to expect that those around him would take care of him. Your mother, a competent and controlling woman, stepped in where his family left off. During your childhood, your father seldom lifted a finger to help around the house, dismissing much of what your mother did as "women's work." Your mother, for the most part, enjoyed being in control and made a joke out of his incompetence. "Give your father a dish to dry, and he'll probably break it," she would say derisively. He, in turn, would ignore her remarks and continue reading his newspaper.

As your parents aged, this pattern continued, although your mother was clearly struggling with the day-to-day tasks she once did with ease. You encouraged them to get some outside help, but your mother said she could manage, and your father said that he didn't want strangers in the house.

One morning, about a year ago, you got a frantic call from your father. Your mother had suffered a stroke and was in intensive care. The months that followed were a nightmare. Your mother spent several weeks in a hospital and then another two months in a nursing home before she died. During that time, your father was beside himself. Not only was he facing the loss of his wife of 50 years, but he had no idea how to take care of things at home. You stopped by daily to keep him company, to prepare his meals, and to keep the house in shape. (Given his level of distress, you didn't have the heart to hire outside help and bring strangers into your father's home.) Even after your mother died, you continued to drop in several times a week, partly out of habit and partly out of a reluctance to confront your father about reducing the amount of time you spent taking care of him. Now, more than a year later, you are still shopping, cooking, doing his laundry, and cleaning for him—just as your mother did.

In the meantime, your own family life has begun to suffer. At least three days a week you rush home, throw dinner together, and spend the entire evening trying to catch up on your own chores. Your husband, who supported your efforts and willingly helped out around the house at first, has now become angry. "You're his daughter, not his wife," he complains. "Tell your father that I matter, too." You have tried to satisfy your husband by doing as much as possible for your father before you go to work, but there are only so many hours available. Mealtime is still an issue at home, and socializing has all but ground to a halt. You simply haven't the energy to do much in the evenings but sleep. During the past month the situation at home has deteriorated further: now your husband and you are hardly talking. You know that your father will be angry with you if you stop taking care of him, but you fear for your marriage if you don't.

Clarify the Problem

1. Does everyone agree a problem exists?

You and your husband clearly see that a problem exists. Your father does not.

2. How urgent is the problem, really?

The problem is fairly urgent. Although your father's health and safety are not at risk, your marriage is. Your husband has essentially said, "You have to choose between him and me." So, you need to find a way to manage your father's care and still have a life.

3. What is behind your father's problematic behavior?

Once your mother died, you inherited 50 years of your father's bad habits. Regardless of his actual level of competence, your father has come to expect being waited on hand and foot. Your mother fostered his dependency, which effectively prevented him from learning how to take care of himself in any significant way. Since both your parents resisted having anyone but your mother take care of the house, your father is used to family only. In addition, he apparently has little regard for "women's work" or any appreciation of what it entails and is probably unaware of the tremendous effort involved in all you do for him.

4. What's hooking you?

Your father's dependency, along with your need to be a "good" daughter, have gotten you into this predicament. By remaining incompetent, your father manipulates you into doing everything for him and puts you in the exact same position your mother was in. On top of that, he takes you for granted. Out of compassion for your father, you are perpetuating the same pattern that existed in his 50-year marriage.

5. Who must be included in problem-solving discussions?

Your father and you are the ones who have to work out this problem. Only then can you and your husband begin solving the problems you are facing in your marriage.

6. What is your goal?

You want to make sure your father's needs are taken care of without jeopardizing your marriage.

Solve the Problem

1. Decide on the needs your solution must satisfy.

Your solution must ensure that your father has food to eat, a clean house, and clean clothing. It must be acceptable to him, especially since he is so resistant to change. It must also allow you to spend sufficient time with your husband to repair the damage to your marriage. Finally, it must satisfy your own need for relief.

2. Come up with a few possible solutions.

One solution is for you to continue to perform some of the tasks your father needs done, while insisting that he learn, with your help, how to do the rest. Another solution is to use outside resources for some or all of your father's needs. For example, you or your father can hire someone to clean and do laundry once a week. You can arrange for food delivery from a supermarket, or purchase prepared meals.

3. Analyze the choices and select the best solution.

(See chart on opposite page.)

The best solution is to insist that your father learn how to take care of some of his own needs, since it lightens your load and avoids problems that can come from using outside help.

4. Conduct a Murphy's Law analysis.

Since your father has never taken care of himself, he is not likely to welcome this option, at least not at first. You will have to be persistent and stand firm about your need to limit the time you spend taking care of him. To make this transition less daunting to him, you can ease him into it by introducing a task and giving him needed instruction in small doses.

If your father refuses to take care of himself at all, and you have made it clear that you can't do everything for him, he may grudgingly agree to the idea of accepting help from strangers. A

GOAL: How can I meet my father's needs and still have time for my husband?

NEEDS	POSSIBLE SOLUTIONS		
	Do nothing	Have your father take care of some of his own needs	Use outside resources to take care of some or all of your father's needs
Must ensure that your father has food to eat and a clean house and clothes	yes	yes	yes
Must meet your father's approval	yes	not sure how he will feel about this	not sure how he will feel about this
Must allow you to spend time with your husband	no	yes	yes
Must satisfy your need for relief	no	yes	yes

laundry service or a supermarket that delivers will be the logical starting place. You can work with him to arrange for these services and help him learn to use them. However, you will have to be sure he understands that you expect him eventually to handle these tasks himself.

If your father is truly obstinate and insists that only you can take care of him the way your mother did, you will have to spell out what you can and cannot do for him—and then stick to your plan. Setting these limits, however, will almost certainly trigger some guilt. "How can I do this to my father?" you may ask yourself.

There are two things you can do to avoid letting your guilt cause you to slip back into old patterns. The first is to remind yourself that *you* are not doing anything to *him* but that *he* is inadvertently exploiting *you*. The second is to ask your husband and friends to help you maintain perspective. If necessary, join a support group of others who are providing care for elderly parents, or see a qualified mental health professional for support.

5. Carry out your plan.

Begin by letting your husband know what you are planning to do. Tell him that your goal is to reduce dramatically the time you spend caring for your father by having him take more responsibility for himself. Until your father learns how to do this, however, you will still have to spend a fair amount of time with him. Your husband needs to understand and accept this.

Next, talk with your father about your need to cut down on the time you spend taking care of him. You might say something like, "Dad, I know you've been having a tough time since Mom died, especially since she took care of everything. I've been trying to fill her shoes, but I can't keep going this way. I still want to see you, and I don't mind helping out, but I can't do it all anymore." Avoid bringing your husband's feelings into the discussion. The last thing you need is to put yourself between these two men and have the issue become "Who is more important to you?"

You can tell your father what you are willing to do, either in terms of time or specific tasks, and then bring up the idea of his taking on some of the other tasks himself. Anticipate that he will object. When he does, you might say, "Dad, I know you've never wanted to do this, but you really have no choice. If I can't do it, and you won't do it, you'll have to hire someone else who will do it." If he concedes, discuss which tasks he might be willing to take on. Offer to help him get started. For example, your father might absolutely refuse to cook but could tolerate shopping. If that is the case, you can help him make a shopping list and go to the supermarket with him. (Be sure to include prepared meals and frozen dinners on the list.) Pick a time of day when the store is not likely to be crowded to minimize the number of things he can complain about.

If your father is willing to learn to do laundry, you can teach him how to use the washer and dryer. Show him how to separate the darks from the whites and how much detergent to use. Do this with him a few times until you think he is comfortable. Don't expect him to be gracious or appreciative, but with your encouragement, he may eventually enjoy his self-sufficiency.

6. Evaluate your progress.

You will know your plan is working if your father takes on enough of his own care that you have some relief. Another indicator, of course, is that your husband is satisfied that you have not abandoned him, and you no longer feel that your marriage is in jeopardy.

༈

My mother won't discuss
end-of-life issues.

Situation

Your widowed mother turned 80 a month ago. She is diabetic and has had a series of mild strokes over the past year. You and your brother are concerned about her failing health and would like to know her wishes about end-of-life care. She has no living will and has not named a health care proxy. Your father was never willing to discuss advance directives, which made his death much more difficult for the family than was necessary. Both you and your brother thought that experience would convince your mother of the importance of making her wishes clear. However, to your surprise, whenever the two of you bring up these topics, she adamantly refuses to discuss them.

Clarify the Problem

1. Does everyone agree a problem exists?

Although you and your brother consider it essential that your mother decide how she wants to be cared for during the final days of her life, your mother's position is, "I don't want to talk about this." While you cannot *make* her talk with you, it would clearly be in everyone's best interest to break through this impasse.

2. How urgent is the problem, really?

Although there is no imminent crisis, your mother's age and failing health make it unwise to postpone decisions. Moreover, her mind is sound at present, and she is fully capable of conveying her wishes to you. This may change at any time.

3. What is behind your mother's problematic behavior?

Because of your mother's experience with your father's death, you know that she is only too aware of the importance of having a living will, naming a health care proxy, and completing a durable power of attorney for health care. Why, then, is she so resistant? Her opposition most likely stems from fear. Talking about advance directives inevitably raises the specter of death. It is little wonder she resists doing it.

There is likely one other reason as well. Many seniors don't like to "jinx" themselves by talking about death, fearing that if they talk about it, it will happen.

4. What's hooking you?

It is an awesome responsibility to oversee the death of a loved one, and it is understandable that you want to know your mother's wishes. Nevertheless, insisting that she talk about end-of-life care so that *you* will feel more comfortable is a little like telling someone to put on a sweater because *you're* chilly.

In addition, you and your brother can hardly be neutral about discussing your mother's death. This is your mother, after all, and you have a very personal stake in her living. Most people have to steel themselves to talk about these matters with someone they love. Your mother could be sensing your discomfort and be trying to spare both of you emotionally by refusing to talk about the issues that are concerning you.

5. Who must be included in problem-solving discussions?

We recommend that only those people who are directly involved be included: your mother, you, and your brother. Involving well-meaning outsiders, each with their own biases, can create difficulties. The clergy, for example, might argue against advance directives, preferring to see matters of life and death left in the hands of God. Your mother's physician might argue that it is his or her duty to prolong life at all possible costs. Hearing this advice from such influential people might close the door on a meaningful discussion of the various options available to your mother, if she were inclined to discuss them.

6. What is your goal?

Your goal is to overcome your mother's resistance to talking about end-of-life issues. You also want her to express her wishes clearly by completing the appropriate formal documents. These must be properly executed and witnessed. Such written documents hold the best possibility of being respected by physicians. (See *Advance Directives* on opposite page.)

Solve the Problem

1. Decide on the needs your solution must satisfy.

First, your solution must help your mother overcome her reluctance to talk about how she wants to be cared for at the end of her life.

Second, since she has already said she will not talk about this topic, your solution must make it possible for her to change her mind without losing face or dignity. This means that regardless of how you feel, you must avoid statements like "It's about time" or "I'm glad you've decided to be reasonable," which will only hurt or anger her.

Third, your solution must let her know that you are prepared to discuss the reality of her death and that she does not need to protect you from such a discussion.

Finally, your solution must enable her to express her wishes clearly, preferably in a way that will have legal standing.

Advance Directives

For information about advance directives, as well as to obtain blank forms that fulfill the legal requirements of all fifty states, contact:

US LIVING WILL REGISTRY, (800) 548-9455, www.uslivingwillregistry.com.

Forms and information are also available from physicians, hospitals, senior centers, and many local libraries.

A copy of your parent's advance directive should be sent to your parent's physician. The documents need to be updated periodically—some suggest annually—if they are to be taken seriously by medical professionals.

2. Come up with a few possible solutions.

Regardless of how you want to resolve your dilemma, you must first confront your mother about her refusal to speak about end-of-life issues and let her know how this is affecting you. If fear of facing death is part of her reluctance, she may need to be reassured that she will not die sooner just because she talks about it.

Confrontation alone, however, is not enough. Your mother also needs to act. An oral statement to you of her wishes will provide you with some guidance on what to ask for if a medical emergency arises, but in the absence of a written document, it can be difficult to persuade attending physicians that you know your mother's wishes and are conveying them accurately.

Your mother can also tell her doctor or other health care provider what her wishes are. This will carry more weight than a statement made to members of the family, since her health care providers will be speaking as objective professionals, but, again, it lacks any legal standing.

If your mother is not comfortable talking to you or her physician, she can make her wishes known by writing them down in a letter to you and your brother. Although this choice will have little legal standing as well (and you should let your mother know that), it can serve as a first step. Having broken the ice, she may be more willing to complete and sign the proper documents at a later time.

Finally, the approach that has the most legal standing is for your mother to complete and sign the necessary legal forms.

3. Analyze the choices and select the best solution.

GOAL: How can I get my mother to talk about end-of-life issues?

	POSSIBLE SOLUTIONS		
NEEDS	Do nothing	Confront and inform your mother, but let her choose her own way of making her wishes known	Confront and inform your mother, and have her complete and sign the needed documents
Must help your mother overcome her reluctance to discuss how she wishes to be cared for at the end of her life	no	yes	yes
Must allow your mother to change her mind about talking to you and telling you her wishes without losing face	no	yes, if you are tactful	yes, if you are tactful
Must convey that you are not afraid to face your mother's death	no	yes	yes
Must have legal standing and therefore be likely to be respected	no	probably not	yes

Confronting and informing your mother, and having her complete and sign the appropriate documents is the preferred solution, since it not only informs you of her wishes but has legal standing as well.

4. Conduct a Murphy's Law analysis.

Once your mother has started to talk, she may shut down again. Something someone says may frighten her or cause her to retreat. For example, she may speak with a friend who thinks your mother is making a mistake. If that happens, you will need to talk to her about her friend's motivations and reassure her of the soundness of her own choice.

Your mother may read something in a magazine or newspaper that gives her second thoughts. For example, someone may have written an article stating that advance directives are sometimes ignored by doctors. If this happens, let her air her concerns, and then find information that will provide her with a more balanced picture. You can also remind her that by not signing the forms, she increases the chances of getting care that runs contrary to her wishes.

5. Carry out your plan.

To overcome your mother's refusal to talk about matters, it might help to let her know how this is affecting you. You might say something like this: "Mom, I know you don't want to discuss this. It's very uncomfortable for all of us. Larry and I can't force you to talk about something against your will, but we're very concerned. We know that you may not die for many years, but regardless of when it happens, we will eventually have to deal with it. When that time comes, we want to ensure that your wishes are respected, and we can't do that without knowing what they are." By openly sharing your distress and sadness at the thought of losing her, you tell her that you care and that you have the strength to address the issue of her death.

This approach is useful for three reasons:

- By acknowledging her discomfort about talking, and letting her know you share that discomfort, you are reminding her that you and your brother are on the same side she is.

- By admitting that you cannot force her to speak, you are showing respect for her feelings. At the same time, you are allowing her to change her mind—if only for the sake of her children—without losing face.

- By being clear about why you need to know her wishes, your request will make more sense to her, and she will be more likely to comply.

Assuming that you have been successful in overcoming your mother's reluctance to talk, you can make things easier for her by listening sensitively. (Guidelines for listening appear on pages 11–12.) Have the actual documents you need on hand—forms for a living will, for naming a health care proxy, etc.—and instructions for completing them. Seeing what is actually involved may be less frightening than talking in the abstract. Give your mother time to look them over. Ask her when she would like to sign the documents and whom she would prefer as witnesses. Once she has agreed, you can then arrange for the papers to be signed, witnessed, and kept with her medical records.

6. Evaluate your progress.

You have succeeded when your mother willingly signs the necessary documents. Since she may not make the decision all at once, you can use the following milestones to chart your progress. You will know you are moving in the right direction when the following occur:

- Your mother's refusal to talk about death is less insistent.

- Your mother is willing to talk perhaps just a little bit and under very limited conditions.

- Your mother lets you know she is willing to discuss only certain subjects (such as a "do not resuscitate" order) but not others.

- Your mother starts acknowledging a range of emotions as she contemplates the end of her life.
- Your mother agrees to express her preferences about end-of-life care.

If you can't get your mother to talk at all, you can strengthen your case by combing magazines, newspapers, and TV listings for stories, articles, and programs that might persuade her to reconsider her refusal. Even if you ultimately fail, you'll have made the strongest case you can. You owe it to her and to yourself to do no less.

༶

My mother can't manage her checking account any longer, but she refuses my help.

Situation

Your mother was widowed unexpectedly five years ago at the age of 81. Although your father had always been the one responsible for managing the family finances, your mother decided after his death that she wanted to take on the job herself. You supported her decision, since it would keep her mind active and provide her with a sense of self-sufficiency. Moreover, you knew the task was not a difficult one. Her Social Security check was deposited electronically. The only bills she had to pay were routine monthly ones, an annual payment on her homeowner's insurance, and occasional miscellaneous expenses. You helped her open her own checking account and asked a bank representative to show her how to write checks and balance her checkbook.

She managed well until last year when her bank was taken over by a large, interstate banking corporation. The new checks and different account number were confusing to her. You explained the changes to her at the time and reassured her; she seemed fine. Then the new monthly statement arrived. It was different from the one she was used to, and she had trouble making sense of it—although she did not tell you. You learned later that she attempted to reach her local branch, but the number was not listed. And when she tried the bank's 800 number, she was thoroughly stymied by the recorded menus and hung up in despair.

To complicate matters, in the past year your mother has had several major, unexpected expenses, including a roof repair and a new hot water heater. All these simultaneous changes were too much for her to cope with. As a result of her confusion, she lost track of her electronic deposits, failed to maintain the necessary minimum balance in her account, and bounced several checks. The bank began sending her warning letters and imposed service charges. Creditors began calling and frightening her, and she started receiving letters from collection agencies.

Last week she called you, anxious and upset about yet another threatening letter. You offered to help her, but your discussions have been frustrating. Each time you try to balance her checkbook with her, she becomes sullen and noncooperative. She is angry at the bad service she received from the bank. She is also impatient with your efforts. Although it would be simpler for you to take charge of her finances, when you offered to do so, your mother became furious. "It's not me!" she said in self-defense. "This new bank is just awful! I can't keep track of all these new numbers!"

Clarify the Problem

1. Does everyone agree a problem exists?

Phone calls and letters from your mother's bank and creditors have let both of you know there is a problem, so there is no denying something is wrong. However, your mother considers the problem the bank's confusing system rather than her own inability to cope with the changes.

2. How urgent is the problem, really?

While this isn't a matter of physical health or safety, it is a problem that needs to be taken seriously. Not only is your mother's financial well-being at stake, so is her peace of mind. Unless a solution can be found, she will come away from this experience feeling disheartened, perhaps even anxious and depressed about her inability to manage this aspect of her life.

3. What is behind your mother's problematic behavior?

There are reasons your mother will not voluntarily give up control of her checkbook. Unless you uncover them and learn why she is fighting you on this point, it is unlikely you will be able to resolve the dilemma to her satisfaction and yours.

Consider that there was something symbolic about her taking over responsibility for her own finances after your father's death. It might have been her way of declaring her competence and her desire to remain independent. Giving up the management of her checking account would be a major blow to her self-esteem, a sign that she is not competent and needs to be taken care of.

Often seniors are reluctant to surrender responsibility for their finances because of the sense of security that accompanies being in control of their money. Your mother may feel that as long as she has control of her spending, nobody can tell her what to do or how to live.

4. What's hooking you?

It is understandable that you are concerned about your mother's financial problems as well as her emotional distress. However, you might also be embarrassed by your mother's errors, imagining that they are somehow a reflection on you—an indication of your failure to take care of her properly. You may also worry that you will be held liable by the bank if you do not solve the problem right away.

5. Who needs to be included in problem-solving discussions?

It is up to you and your mother to find a way of resolving this dilemma. Bank personnel care only that her account be managed properly, although they may be willing to help to some extent. Nevertheless, the problem is not theirs. Your mother's creditors have no real interest in anything other than getting paid.

6. What is your goal?

A successful resolution of this dilemma will allow your mother to maintain control of her finances, including paying her bills correctly and on time.

Solve the Problem

1. Decide on the needs your solution must satisfy.

The solution you decide on must eliminate or sharply reduce your mother's checking account errors and do so without damaging her self-esteem. It must also allow her to take care of her checking account by herself.

2. Come up with a few possible solutions.

One option is to speak with a bank representative at the local branch, explain the problem, and ask him or her to meet with your mother and you. At this meeting the representative can suggest ways to help your mother keep track of her account, such as using checks that make duplicate copies. (A bank interested in doing business with your mother should be willing to help out. If you get the impression that bank personnel have no desire to help, find another bank. Even though this will mean a whole new set of numbers for your mother, it will be worth it in the long run.)

Another solution might be to convince your mother to allow you to share responsibility for her checking account until she gets used to the new bank statements and establishes a rhythm again. Have her promise to let you know immediately if she encounters unexpected expenses or becomes confused for any reason, even after the period of shared responsibility ends. Focused, short-term help under these extraordinary circumstances may be all she needs.

As a last resort, you can take complete control of her account, but this will deal a blow to her self-esteem and, therefore, is the least desirable alternative.

3. Analyze the choices and select the best solution.

GOAL: How can I ensure my mother's bills get paid correctly and on time?

POSSIBLE SOLUTIONS				
NEEDS	Do nothing	Have your mother manage her own account with the help of bank personnel	Share responsibility with your mother for managing her account	Take responsibility for your mother's account
Must reduce or eliminate errors in managing her checking account	no	probably	yes	yes
Must allow your mother to retain her self-esteem	no	yes	yes, if done sensitively	no
Must allow your mother to retain complete control of her money	yes	yes	no	no

Based on this analysis, the optimal solution is for your mother to retain control of her account with the help of bank personnel.

4. Conduct a Murphy's Law analysis.

The success of your plan depends primarily on the willingness of bank personnel to answer your mother's questions and respond to her concerns. If bank staffing changes, you will need to be sure that everyone understands the arrangement and agrees to continue providing help.

Arranging for checks that give your mother duplicate copies will solve the problem of keeping track of checks she has written, but it does not help her keep track of electronic deposits. You may need to add some additional procedures for her to follow, such as recording the deposits in her check register on a predetermined day of the month.

You may also need to intervene when you learn about an extraordinary expense that may upset your mother's check-writing routine. At these times you may need to help out to prevent your mother from being thrown off track.

If nothing works to eliminate your mother's confusion, you will have no choice but to share responsibility for managing the account. Ultimately, you may need to take it over completely.

5. Carry out your plan.

Since the immediate problem is to clear up the mess that already exists, the first step in carrying out your plan is to find out the exact status of your mother's account. Specifically, what is her balance? What checks have yet to clear? Next, you will want to call her creditors and explain what has occurred. Find out what is owed to them and formulate a payment plan to settle her accounts.

Then, arrange a meeting with your mother and a bank representative. Help them to review the problem together and plan the steps that can be taken to eliminate or reduce errors. For example, the bank representative can show your mother how to read her monthly statement and can issue her a checkbook that provides duplicate copies. By the end of the meeting, your mother should understand what procedures to follow. If she doesn't, ask for a set of written instructions, and arrange for an additional meeting if necessary. Make sure she has the name and phone number of the representative in case she has any questions or runs into a problem.

If you are ordering new checks, help your mother use her old ones until the new ones arrive. (Make clear that this involvement is only temporary.) Once she takes over, secure her permission to oversee her account until you are satisfied that she fully understands the procedures she is to follow.

Keep the bank's representative informed about how things are progressing. Your involvement lightens the representative's load and helps ensure future cooperation.

6. Evaluate your progress.

If the plan you choose is working, your mother will no longer be making errors with her checking account. A rhythm will develop, with routine bills coming in and being paid promptly and correctly. Should this *not* occur, pinpoint the cause of the problem by reviewing your mother's statements and check register and by speaking with the bank and her creditors. If nothing works and independent management of her checkbook is truly beyond your mother's ability, you will need to step in and become more involved.

DILEMMA TWELVE

୬

My sister volunteered to take care of my mother, and now she refuses to let me help.

Situation

Your widowed mother, now 80, had a stroke a year ago. Although her mind was not affected, she never recovered her physical mobility, and she remains wheelchair bound. She is unable to cook, clean, or shop for herself.

At the time of her stroke, you were involved in a major project at work and were grateful when your younger sister, Eileen, who lives near your mother, offered to take care of her. It also made sense, initially, for Eileen rather than you to take charge because she does not work (she receives alimony) or have children. You assumed that as soon as your schedule became more manageable, you would do your share and give Eileen some relief. However, when you were able to help and offered to do so, your sister, with whom you've never had a particularly close relationship, was not receptive.

Eileen currently spends most of every day with your mother and does all the shopping and home chores. She calls your mother in the evenings as well. Even though you devote most of your time to your family and career, you still want to do your share for your mother. However, whenever you offer to help, Eileen says no. You have suggested that at least you can cover for her on weekends, but Eileen is not interested. Despite her opposition, you have tried to become involved. For example, you once bought a gripper device for your mother to make it easier for her to turn faucets on and off by herself. After having your mother try it out, Eileen pronounced it unnecessary. The next time you visited, it had disappeared.

Eileen is clearly elbowing you out by limiting your involvement to visiting and having a cup of coffee. You are stymied and feeling increasingly resentful toward her.

Clarify the Problem

1. Does everyone agree a problem exists?

Neither your mother nor your sister is complaining. Eileen is meeting your mother's needs and obviously wants to take care of her by herself. You are the only one who thinks there is a problem.

2. How urgent is the problem, really?

There is no real urgency here. Your mother's health and well-being are not at risk. Eileen is happy. You are distressed, however, feeling excluded and wanting very much to see that change.

3. What is behind your sister's problematic behavior?

There are undeniably good and practical reasons for Eileen to have taken over your mother's care, and she is certainly doing a competent job. However, caregiving may be serving her interests at some expense to both your mother and you. Eileen has little to do with her time, and providing care may be giving her life a meaning and a purpose it would otherwise lack. At the same time, in her zeal, she may be doing more than necessary, which can foster your mother's dependency on her. While this guarantees Eileen's continued role as caregiver, it prevents your mother from becoming as self-reliant as she might.

Additionally, Eileen's not allowing you a caregiving role deprives your mother of the pleasure of receiving your help and deprives you of the satisfaction of providing it. Eileen is trying to deny you your role in the family. Since the two of you have never been very close, it is highly likely there is a rivalry between you. As your younger sister, she may never have felt she could outdo you. Your mother's disability now gives her the chance to do so. Moreover, her life has apparently not gone well. You have the satisfactions of an intact marriage, children, and a career. She has none of these. It would not be surprising if she is seizing this opportunity to lord it over you. Given your competence, she may fear that if you play *any* part in your mother's care, you will take it over.

While you can't be certain your mother is contributing to the problem by not insisting that Eileen allow you to help, your mother may be going along with your sister's game of one-upmanship. On the other hand, it is possible that your mother is assuming you are too busy with your own life to become involved.

4. What's hooking you?

What bothers you most is that you are being deprived of the opportunity to demonstrate that you are a caring daughter. Moreover, you are losing your sense of your place in the family. Eileen enjoys the status of caregiver and has cast you in the role of a person with nothing of value to offer. (You are a mere visitor when you drop by to see your mother—much as a neighbor would be.) You may also be concerned about what others are thinking. "Eileen is doing everything," you can imagine them saying, "while her sister just drops in from time to time."

5. Who must be included in problem-solving discussions?

You and Eileen certainly need to be included. Depending on your mother's awareness of the problem, she may need to be included as well.

6. What is your goal?

Your goal is to get Eileen to share responsibility for your mother's care with you.

Solve the Problem

1. Decide on the needs your solution must satisfy.

Your solution must meet your need to help provide care for your mother. It must also ensure that your mother continues to receive adequate care. Finally, it must be acceptable to Eileen, since without her cooperation your solution cannot work.

2. Come up with a few possible solutions.

Eileen does not want to hand over control of the caregiving to you. Therefore, one solution is to find ways to help that do not threaten her. Tell her, for example, that you want to do some shopping for your mother before your next visit, and ask Eileen to make up a list. In that way, she still has some control, which may allow her to come to terms more easily with your involvement. Once she sees you are not threatening to take over, you can gradually incorporate more activities.

A second option is to have a three-way discussion about your mother's care. Make it clear that you want to be more involved, and ask your mother and Eileen to suggest ways you can do that. In your mother's presence, Eileen may be less likely to object to your involvement.

A third possibility is to invite your mother to spend a few days with you and your family. You will have to work out the practical considerations, such as whether your home can be made wheelchair accessible and whether you can take the time off from work. If your mother is eager to visit, it will be hard for Eileen to stand in your way. If the visit goes well, and your mother realizes how willing you are to help, she may become an ally in encouraging Eileen to share the caregiving.

3. Analyze your choices and select the best solution.

(See chart on opposite page.)

Starting to take on small tasks when you visit your mother is the best preliminary solution. As a limited change, it is the least

GOAL: How can I get my sister to let me share responsibility for taking care of our mother?

	POSSIBLE SOLUTIONS			
NEEDS	Do nothing	Start to take on small tasks when you come to visit your mother	Have a three-way talk with your mother and sister about how you can help out	Have your mother spend a few days with you and your family
Must meet your need to become actively involved in your mother's care	no	yes	yes	yes
Must maintain an adequate level of care for your mother	yes	yes	yes	yes
Must be acceptable to your sister	yes	possibly, since your sister will still be in charge of your mother's care	possibly, since your sister will still be in charge of your mother's care	probably not

threatening to Eileen and will allow her to remain in control of your mother's care. It also carries the potential for more involvement on your part.

4. Conduct a Murphy's Law analysis.

The biggest possible obstacle to your incorporating some tasks into your social visits is Eileen's refusal to let you do anything. If she is completely against it, prevail on her to discuss the matter with both you and an impartial third party. This could be a trusted member of the clergy, friend, relative, or therapist. If Eileen still refuses, and your mother is unaware of what is going on, you may want to ask your mother's help. At the very least, she will see that you are willing to take care of her.

There is another possibility. Suppose Eileen responds to your complaint by saying, "Fine. You want to help? Then *you* take care of Mom." Since you are clearly not able to do this, you have little choice but to back down for the time being. Your mother's well-being is a higher priority than your pride.

5. Carry out your plan.

No matter what solution you choose, you need to let Eileen know how important it is to you to become involved. This conversation will be difficult since you have to tell her the effect her behavior is having on you without blaming or provoking her (see pages 12–13 for help in using *I*-messages). "I feel terrible," you might say. "When I visit Mom, I feel like a neighbor or a total stranger, not her daughter! I know you're working hard to take care of Mom, and everyone appreciates that. But I'm feeling irrelevant, and that hurts. I really need you to let me do more. She's my mother, too."

You will also have to acknowledge that the two of you have never had an ideal relationship and insist that it not stand in the way of your right to take care of your mother. "I know we've never been close," you might say, "but this is *our* mother we're talking about. And I have a right and a need to be involved in her care, too. No matter how well you've been able to care for her by yourself, I have something to offer as well. Let's find a way to work together." By fostering an attitude of cooperation, it might be possible to soften Eileen's opposition.

As you speak, you need to keep in mind Eileen's fear that you, her big sister, will take over if allowed to get your foot in the door. It will be reassuring to remind her that she will remain at the center of things even when you do become involved.

6. Evaluate your progress.

You will know you have succeeded when you are satisfied with your contribution to your mother's care.

cs?

My father refuses to wear his hearing aids, even though he insisted on getting them.

Situation

Your 70-year-old father, who was widowed in his 50s, began losing his hearing several years ago. Although his condition was mild at first, it grew steadily worse over the years. Being an outgoing and social man, his inability to hear caused him great embarrassment and distress. You found it hard to talk with him, both in person and by phone. One day several months ago, he told you he had spoken with his friends at the senior center and learned that many of them found hearing aids useful. As a result of his findings, he asked your help in getting himself fitted for one. You agreed.

Although willing to help, you were dismayed to discover that all the participating providers under your father's health insurance plan were located quite a distance from you. Three trips back and forth for testing and fitting required a significant commitment on your part. Fortunately, the audiologist was convinced that hearing aids for both ears would help your father. Unfortunately, the audiologist strongly recommended a top-of-the-line model, which was only partially covered by the insurance. Since your father could not afford the aids, you offered to pay $2000 out of your own pocket.

When your father first wore his new hearing aids three

months ago, everyone noticed an immediate and marked improvement. You and your entire family were able to converse normally with him. He seemed happy, too, remarking that he enjoyed being with his friends again. Imagine your surprise and chagrin, though, when two weeks later you found out your father was refusing to wear the hearing aids. "They're damned uncomfortable," he reported, when you asked him why he had stopped. "And they don't help much anyway!"

Clarify the Problem

1. Does everyone agree a problem exists?

There is more than one problem here. Your father's inability to hear is one. His refusal to wear the aids that can solve the problem is the other. Your father acknowledges he has trouble hearing, a fact confirmed by anyone else with whom he must interact. However, he is unwilling to accept the discomfort he feels, and he thinks the hearing aids are not as effective as he expected. For him, wearing the aids is a greater problem than not hearing well.

You, on the other hand, don't want to see things regress. Once again you dread what it will be like trying to have a conversation with him. You are also concerned that he will be embarrassed and frustrated in social settings and will consequently avoid them.

2. How urgent is the problem, really?

This is not an urgent problem. However, the effects of hearing loss are serious, including social isolation and mistrust of others, who seem to be talking behind one's back. Therefore, the situation should not be allowed to go on for long.

3. What is behind your father's problematic behavior?

Your father's refusal to wear the hearing aids comes from many sources. The aids are uncomfortable. He may have expected not to feel the devices at all. Even though the aids are tiny, people do feel them in their ears until they get used to them.

He also claims they don't help much, which may mean either that he must learn to adjust them and use them properly or that he is experiencing a kind of sensory overload that he finds disconcerting and unacceptable.

In addition, he may feel self-conscious, despite having *asked* for the aids and despite having friends who wear them. For some people any visible evidence of aging, such as a hearing aid or a cane, is a source of embarrassment.

4. What's hooking you?

Your frustration with your father stems primarily from the fact that you went through considerable inconvenience and personal expense to have him tested and fitted for hearing aids that he now refuses to wear. It is even more frustrating since he thought they were helping at first. You also worry about what will happen if he withdraws socially as his hearing worsens. Adding insult to injury, getting the aids was *his* idea in the first place, not yours.

5. Who must be included in problem-solving discussions?

Your father and you must be included.

6. What is your goal?

You want your father to wear his hearing aids, for his sake and for the sake of those close to him.

Solve the Problem

1. Decide on the needs your solution must satisfy.

Your solution must overcome your father's objections to wearing the aids. It must also satisfy you that he is giving them a fair chance.

2. Come up with a few possible solutions.

The simplest solution is to contact the audiologist, explain what has happened, and ask for his help. A second solution is to ask one of your father's hearing-impaired friends to talk with him about the difficulties he or she had adjusting to hearing aids. Finally, you might locate books or articles on hearing aids that discuss problems encountered by new users and the solutions to those problems. You could give the reading material to your father or plan on going over it together. (See *Hearing Loss and Treatment* on opposite page.)

3. Analyze the choices and select the best solution.

GOAL: How can I get my father to wear his hearing aids?

	POSSIBLE SOLUTIONS			
NEEDS	Do nothing	Enlist the help of the audiologist who fit your father	Enlist the help of one of your father's friends	Give your father reading material about hearing aids and new users of them
Must overcome your father's objections	no	probably	probably	possibly
Must satisfy you that your father has given the hearing aids a fair chance	no	yes	probably, if he agrees to a trial period	possibly

Consulting with the audiologist is the best solution because he has the expertise and experience that can be most helpful to your father.

4. Conduct a Murphy's Law analysis.

If your father is adamant about not wearing his hearing aids, he might refuse to come with you to the audiologist. You might be able to work around his resistance if you assure him that seeing the audiologist will not obligate him to wear the hearing aids. Remind your father that he really wanted the aids and liked

Hearing Loss and Treatment

One of the best recent books on hearing loss is Richard Carmen's *Consumer Handbook on Hearing Loss and Hearing Aids: A Bridge to Healing*, 2nd ed (Sedona, AZ: Auricle Ink, 2004). This highly readable work contains essays and advice from some of the nation's leading experts on hearing loss.

For additional information about hearing loss, hearing aids, and related topics, call one of the following organizations. All of them offer guidance and information as well as publications. Some provide advice and assistance on legal issues relating to deafness.

BETTER HEARING INSTITUTE,
(703) 684-3391; www.betterhearing.org/

NATIONAL ASSOCIATION OF THE DEAF,
(301) 587-1789; www.nad.org/

SELF HELP FOR HARD OF HEARING PEOPLE,
(301) 657-2248; www.shhh.org/

them at first. You can also let him know that he is making his own life, and yours, much more difficult. If none of these approaches works, remind him that you invested a great deal to help him, and he owes it to you to give the aids a fair trial.

If your father visits the audiologist but then refuses to follow his recommendations, you can try to find out what is fueling his reluctance, although he may not know himself. At this point, encouraging him to speak with a friend or giving him some reading material about hearing aids might help.

As a last resort, you might let him know how upset you are that he asked for your help and now refuses to give the aids a fair trial. You can remind him that you bent over backwards to accommodate him, and you feel he owes it to both of you to do his share to help himself.

5. Carry out your plan.

Before you talk to your father, call the audiologist, explain what is happening, and ask his advice. He may be able to offer suggestions over the phone about how to proceed. He may also suggest materials you can share with your father. If he recommends a consultation, have him offer some possible meeting times. Speak with your father and have him choose one.

Assuming the meeting with the audiologist occurs and a plan is agreed on, help your father follow the recommendations. This might involve his learning how to use the aids properly, as well as a trial period during which he wears them for increasingly longer periods of time, until he gets used to them.

6. Evaluate your progress.

The measure of your success is clear: If your father makes a good adjustment to the aids, wears them faithfully, and enjoys the benefits of being able to hear, you will know you have succeeded.

My mother treats my brother like a god, but I'm the one who does all the work.

Situation

For the past four years, you have been helping your 90-year-old mother take care of herself so she can continue to live independently. You visit her three times a week and call her almost every day. You do her laundry. You shop and clean for her. You cook most of her meals. You take her to the doctor for routine checkups or when she is ill. You make sure your husband and children visit her. And you keep other relatives informed about how she is doing. (They know that you are the person to call to find out how your mom is.) But you are wearing yourself out caring for her.

Your only sibling is an older brother, who lives an hour away. He maintains a pleasant, although distant, relationship with you and rarely calls or visits. He is not at all involved in the day-to-day care of your mother. Ironically, however, when he does do something for her, your mother beams with pride and cannot praise him enough. For example, when he sent her flowers on Mother's Day, she positively glowed with pleasure. For weeks afterward, she commented on his gift and boasted about her wonderful son to anyone who would listen. On those rare occasions when he visits (twice a year, usually on her birthday and around the holidays), your mother treats him like a god. She even expects you to prepare dinner and to entertain him. You do not dislike your brother, but you feel hurt and resentful that his meager efforts elicit far more praise from your mother than your many efforts do.

Clarify the Problem

1. Does everyone agree a problem exists?

You are the only one who feels there is a problem. Your mother has no idea there is anything amiss. Her day-to-day needs are met with such skill that she simply assumes what needs to be done will be done—by a daughter who asks for very little and whose personal exhaustion and distress are kept neatly inside her.

From your brother's perspective, there is no problem, either. He does virtually nothing, yet he receives accolades for the simplest things. Your mother adores him, while you feel like Cinderella.

2. How urgent is the problem, really?

The urgency in this situation centers around your needs. Put simply, you are at risk for burnout. You already display some of the signs: you are tired and resentful; you feel taken for granted (and rightly so). Yet you have done nothing to improve your situation. Chances are, if you allow things to continue, your resentment will escalate to the point that your health, marriage, and caregiving will suffer.

3. What is behind your mother's and brother's problematic behaviors?

Your mother may feel that taking care of her is your duty as her daughter—and not your brother's responsibility. She doesn't thank you because she may feel no thanks are due. Or she may assume you know she is grateful and may not realize how hurt you feel when she says nothing.

Your mother obviously has a different relationship with your brother. Most likely he has always been her favorite, and everything he does delights her. A look into your family history will probably confirm that her current behavior is simply an old pattern in a new form.

What about your brother's behavior? Like your mother, he may believe that it is your place, not his, to look after her. And since you never ask anything of him, you only reinforce his view. The fact that he rarely contacts you suggests that your relationship leaves much to be desired. He simply may not care about how hard you work. He might even enjoy dumping caregiving duties on you, knowing that he can do so without fear of losing your mother's affection.

4. What's hooking you?

You are running yourself ragged trying to care for your mother, which probably means you have not yet given up the hope that if you try hard enough, she will finally notice your efforts and praise you for them. Telling your mother up front how unappreciated you feel means you will never get the spontaneous gratitude you want. In addition, if you tell her how you feel and she responds by saying that it is your duty to take care of her, not only will you be deprived of what you want but you will probably feel embarrassed for wanting it.

You may not be asking for help from your brother because you are trying to prove that you are the better or more caring child, at least in your own eyes. You may also be accumulating "resentment points" so that one day you can remind your brother of all you did for your mother. If he became involved in helping out, you would lose this dubious advantage.

5. Who must be included in problem-solving discussions?

You really have three separate issues here: your need for relief, your brother's lack of involvement in your mother's care, and your feelings about your mother's lack of appreciation. The first issue—your need for relief—is best handled by a discussion among all three of you. Each of the other two issues can be addressed in a two-way discussion between the person involved and you.

6. What is your goal?

Your immediate goal is to remove yourself from the position of being your mother's sole helper, preferably by involving your brother in caring for her. In addition, you are hoping to lessen the resentment you feel toward your mother and brother. Finally, at some point you would like some appreciation from your mother.

Solve the Problem

1. Decide on the needs your solution must satisfy.

Your solution must reduce the amount of time and energy you spend taking care of your mother. It must also reduce the level of resentment you feel. Your mother's physical and emotional needs must continue to be met. And since you would like your brother's help, your solution should be acceptable to him as well.

2. Come up with a few possible solutions.

Your solution should focus primarily on getting the relief you need from all you do for your mother. The best way to do this is by letting your mother and brother know you need assistance. Decide what help you need, and then speak with your brother about pitching in. For example, you might ask him to do the weekly shopping and share the doctor visits with you.

However, if you need more help than he is willing to provide, another solution is to hire someone to take on some or all of your caregiving duties.

Finally, if the situation presents itself, you may want to talk with your mother about feeling unappreciated. However, this is a separate issue, not part of your immediate problem. As such, it can be tackled at a later time.

3. Analyze the choices and select the best solution.

GOAL: How can I get relief from my caregiving responsibilities?

	POSSIBLE SOLUTIONS			
NEEDS	Do nothing	Talk to your mother and brother about being overloaded; ask your brother to help out	Hire outside help to take over some or all of the caregiving tasks	(optional) Talk to your mother about feeling unappreciated
Must relieve you of some caregiving responsibilities	no	yes, if your brother agrees to help	yes	not directly, but it might make her receptive to your need for help
Must help alleviate your resentment	no	possibly, if your brother is willing to help	yes, if you do not shoulder the financial burden alone	possibly, if she is sensitive to your feelings
Must meet your mother's physical and emotional needs	yes, but not for long	yes, if your brother is willing to help	yes, if you continue to visit (your brother must also take more responsibility for visiting)	yes, if done with sensitivity
Must have your brother's approval	yes	uncertain	uncertain	n/a

The best approach at this time is to let your mother and brother know you have reached a breaking point and ask your brother for his help in sharing responsibilities.

4. Conduct a Murphy's Law analysis.

There are several points at which your attempts to resolve this dilemma can go off track. For one, since confrontation is so out of character for you, you may be unable to speak your mind to your brother or mother. Second, since the problem has gone on for several years and your feelings run quite deep, you might be able to *start* talking but could end up getting so angry or upset that you lose your focus and effectiveness.

To avoid either outcome, it is essential that you prepare for the discussions. Take time to plan what you want to say, so that you convey exactly what is on your mind. Rehearse out loud, so you can hear yourself saying the words. If necessary, enlist your husband's support. (He might help you think through what you want to say or actually come with you when you speak with your mother and brother.)

If the prospect of a face-to-face confrontation is too intimidating, consider writing a letter to each of them in advance of your speaking with them. Once they know what is on your mind, it may be easier for you to talk with them. (We offer several additional communication and confrontation suggestions in chapters 2 and 3.)

Even if you succeed in making it clear that you can't continue to provide help by yourself, your brother may still refuse to participate in your mother's care. At that point you will need to fall back on your next option—hiring outside help.

If your mother refuses to accept help from anyone other than family members, you will need to understand why and do your best to meet her objections. If nothing you do satisfies her, then the only alternative is for you to tell her that she must enter an assisted living facility. Once she realizes this, she may agree to try the outside help.

5. Carry out your plan.

Before speaking with your mother or brother, you must decide which jobs you are willing to keep doing and which ones you are not. Next, let your mother and brother know your feelings and intentions. For these conversations, *I*-messages (see pages 12–13) are especially useful, since you want to air your grievances without antagonizing either of them. Saying to your mother, "I simply can't do this alone anymore" is a clean statement. "You never appreciate anything I do" is a personal attack, bound to evoke a defensive response. Similarly, explaining to your brother, "I get upset when you don't ask how you can help" is a straightforward expression of your feelings. "You're selfish and uncaring" is an invitation to an argument or a walkout.

When you speak with them, be clear that *something* needs to change. Tell your brother that you need his help. Reassure your mother that no matter what happens, her needs will continue to be met. If one of them has trouble accepting what you are saying and becomes abusive or bullying, use *you*-messages to keep the situation under control so that you can get your point across.

The content of your conversations with both of them must center around your inability to continue providing care alone and the tasks your brother could perform to lighten your load. If it becomes clear that outside help is necessary, arrangements have to be made. You—or even better, you and your brother— need to find a good quality home health agency. (See *Choosing a Home Health Agency* on pages 86–87.) You both need to be available to help your mother adapt to the new arrangements. Your familiar presence will make the transition easier.

6. Evaluate your progress.

You will know your plan is succeeding if you are no longer the only one providing care and if you feel less resentful toward your mother and brother. In addition, if you decide to speak with your mother about feeling unappreciated, you will know that you conveyed your message successfully once she expresses some gratitude for your efforts.

❧

My father wants to move in with us, but my husband is against it.

Situation

Since your mother's death two years ago, your 78-year-old father has been living alone in the family home. He is in generally good health, although he developed arthritis when he was in his 60s. His hip has become increasingly painful, and he is having trouble now with day-to-day activities. His physician recently told him that a hip replacement may be necessary in the near future.

Whether or not your father has the hip surgery, you and he know he will need help soon. Unfortunately, you live several hours away and cannot visit often since your work leaves you with little free time. Your father has rather boldly proposed to you that he move in with you and your husband. Your home is modest, but you could set aside a room for him. It would be a sacrifice, but it would be possible.

Your father and your 59-year-old husband, George, have never had a close relationship. The fact that your father spoke with you alone about moving in typifies his lack of respect for George and for the role your husband plays in your life. For his part, George was offended that your father did not speak directly with him. In addition, George plans to retire next year. He is afraid that with your father around all day, he will be expected to take care of him.

You, on the other hand, have always been close to your father, although you sometimes have trouble standing up to him. You don't necessarily object to his moving in and would regret turning him down. However, you don't want to agree to something that will create major problems between you and your husband.

Clarify the Problem

1. Does everyone agree a problem exists?

Everyone agrees there is a problem, but each of you sees it as something different. For your father, the problem is that he needs help. As far as he is concerned, moving in with you is the solution. For your husband, the problem is that your father wants to move in. Given the uneasy relationship between the two of them and your father's lack of respect for George, this living arrangement could be a tremendous source of aggravation for your husband. For you, the problem is that your father *and* your husband cannot seem to find a way to get along with each other. You are squarely in the middle.

2. How urgent is the problem, really?

There is no urgency to have your father move in right away. However, he will soon need some kind of help since he is having difficulty living independently. A decision must be made in the near future.

3. What is behind your father's and husband's problematic behaviors?

Your father's lack of sensitivity to your husband's feelings may stem from his self-centeredness and the strength of his relationship with you. He has assumed that you will welcome him into your home, regardless of how he treats George.

Your husband resents the way he is treated by your father and does not want him moving in, regardless of your concern for your father's worsening condition. George can tolerate your father's behavior for short periods of time, but he does not want to live with it every day. Given the strength of your attachment to your father, George may also fear that he will find himself the "odd man out" in his own home.

4. What's hooking you?

Because of the positions they have taken, your husband and your father are forcing you to choose between them. Your father's needs are unmistakable, and his request is not totally unreasonable. You don't want to turn him down for fear you will compromise your relationship with him and be seen by him as uncaring. Having him move in will also reduce your guilt about not being able to visit him more often, while assuring you that he is being taken care of properly.

However, your husband's feelings are also clear and have a basis in fact. You care about him and do not want to hurt him—or your marriage—by disregarding his wishes.

5. Who must be included in problem-solving discussions?

You, your husband, and your father must all be involved.

6. What is your goal?

You want to make sure your father is being cared for in a way that both you and he consider satisfactory. At the same time, whatever you decide to do must not antagonize your husband or jeopardize your marriage.

Solve the Problem

1. Decide on the needs your solution must satisfy.

Your solution must be acceptable to everyone involved. It needs to ensure your father's health and safety, and must preserve your sound relationship with him. Finally, it must avoid creating dissension between you and your husband.

2. Come up with a few possible solutions.

One possibility is to allow your father to move in for a trial period, say six months, to see whether the arrangement can work. You need to be clear from the outset—whether his living with you turns out to be temporary or permanent—that neither you nor your husband will be directly responsible for your father's care. This means that your father has to be willing to hire and pay for a home health aide if his arthritis worsens or if he needs assistance after surgery. He should retain ownership of his home during the trial period in case things don't work out.

Another possibility is for your father to remain where he is and hire people to help him as needed.

3. Analyze your choices and select the best solution.

(See chart on next page.)

The preferred option is to have your father move in for a trial period.

4. Conduct a Murphy's Law analysis.

Two main problems may arise. First, even after you have warned your father not to treat George disrespectfully, he may continue to do so. You and George will have to be adamant that if this happens, your father will have to move back to his own home. If you present a united front, your father is more likely to take this seriously.

The other problem is that your father may refuse to hire outside help when he needs it. He would, in effect, be blackmailing you into providing care. While it would be difficult to send your ailing father back to his own home, you would have no choice. If your father returned home and still refused to hire help, you would be morally obligated to report him for self-neglect to state authorities. (See pages 70–71 for advice on doing this.)

Many other minor problems—the kind that simply come from living under the same roof—might arise over such issues as what to watch on television or having guests visit. By anticipat-

GOAL: How can my father's needs be met without jeopardizing my marriage?

NEEDS	POSSIBLE SOLUTIONS		
	Do nothing	Allow your father to move in for a trial period; have him hire help as needed	Have your father stay in his own home and hire help as needed
Must be acceptable to you	no	yes	yes
Must be acceptable to your husband	yes	probably, if the trial period is a success	yes
Must be acceptable to your father	no	probably	probably not
Must ensure your father's health and safety	no	yes	yes
Must preserve your relationship with your father	no	yes	probably
Must avoid creating dissension between you and your husband	no	probably, if the trial period is a success	yes

ing these difficulties and working together to reach compromises, you may be able to prevent minor problems from becoming major areas of conflict.

5. Carry out your plan.

You are asking a big favor of your husband, and you must be willing to accept his refusal. Explain why your father's moving in is so important to you, and ask whether he would be willing to try it out for a few months. Work out the details of your plan together until you both are satisfied.

Then you *and* your husband should talk with your father and tell him that you are open to having him move in for a trial period, but if he treats George disrespectfully, he will have to move back home and hire people to provide home care as needed. Remember that you are not likely to change your father's disposition, but you may be able to alter his behavior by making the consequences very clear. Tell him what you are and are not willing to do for him, and what you expect in return. To prevent misunderstandings and hurt feelings, all three of you must decide on such matters as furnishings your father can bring into your home, mealtimes, privacy, vacation plans, television viewing, guests, and payment for adaptations that may be needed such as wheelchair ramps or grab bars.

The matter of your father's needing care must also be fully discussed. "Dad," you might say, "since George and I can't take on the responsibility of caring for you ourselves, let's look for a home health agency now—just in case you need one down the road. That way you can be sure you're taken care of properly if the time comes." (See *Choosing a Home Health Agency* on pages 86–87.) Use his reaction to this suggestion as an indicator of how likely he is to respect your terms. If he is uncooperative at this early stage, choose another option.

Assuming that everything can be agreed on, help your father move in and make sure he has arranged for the care of his own home in his absence.

Expect that you, your husband, and your father will go through a period of adjustment that may last several weeks. During that time, be sure everyone agrees to talk rationally about any problems or irritations that arise, so that small grievances do not become serious issues.

6. Evaluate your progress.

You will know you have succeeded when your husband, your father, and you are satisfied with your living arrangements. Complaints from either of them, distress on your part, or dissension between you and your husband may indicate a need to reconsider your solution.

DILEMMA SIXTEEN

უ⁓

My father insists on taking care of my mother, but he is not able to, and they are both suffering.

Situation

Your father is an 85-year-old retired corporate executive. Your mother, a former school administrator, is 83. They have been married for 62 years. Three years ago a stroke left your mother partially paralyzed, and your father became her caregiver. He bathes and dresses her and helps her manage other day-to-day tasks. He also cooks, cleans, and does the laundry. Your mother seems content to have him care for her, and he has managed well for the past few years.

Recently, however, his arthritis has worsened and he looks tired and distressed. Although he seems to be wearing down, he insists he is doing fine. Lately you have noticed that their home is not as clean as it once was. There are dust balls in the corners of rooms, and the bathroom looks as though it hasn't been touched in a long time. There is little food in the house, and what you do find is predominantly frozen dinners, snack foods, and ice cream—foods that are not particularly nutritious but are easy to prepare. In addition, your parents, previously a well-groomed couple, seem dirty and disheveled. Each time you visit, you grow more concerned. However, when you mention getting them some help, both parents become angry.

Clarify the Problem

1. Does everyone agree a problem exists?

Your father has made it clear that he doesn't want any help, and, on the surface, your parents are managing. However, it is wrong to say that no real problem exists. At the very least there is a problem in the making. Your parents' quality of life is deteriorating, and you are right to be concerned.

2. How urgent is the problem, really?

Your parents' diet, home-care, and personal hygiene are your three sources of concern. Although their food is inferior, it is probably adequate. True, their home is not clean and tidy, but it *is* livable. And the decline in their personal hygiene may be unaesthetic, but it does not pose any immediate health risks. No real emergency exists at the moment. However, the situation will continue to deteriorate.

You have a choice to make. You can offer help now, in a way that will not offend them, or you can do nothing at present, but watch for indicators that a crisis is erupting. Here are some possible indicators:

• Your father concedes that he cannot manage any longer.

• Your father neglects or abuses your mother.

• Your mother smells foul for lack of bathing.

• Either or both of your parents begin to lose weight rapidly.

If changes like these occur, it will be difficult to deny that a problem exists. At that point, you will need to intervene, even if it has to be against your parents' wishes.

3. What is behind your parents' problematic behaviors?

Your parents are adamant about not wanting help, even though it is quite apparent they can use it. This tells you there must be powerful motives fueling their resistance. Four possible explanations for their resistance follow.

They are reluctant to admit they can no longer care for themselves. Your offer of help may be heard as a vote of no confidence in your father's ability to care for your mother. He has managed remarkably well, under extremely difficult circumstances, for a long time. Your well-meaning attempt to make his life easier may be heard as a failure to value his efforts and a lack of appreciation for his resourcefulness and competence.

They want to remain independent. Your parents have been capable people all their lives and are used to making their own decisions. It should be no surprise, therefore, that they are resisting your making decisions for them.

They are denying the seriousness of your father's worsening arthritis. Over the years, your father and mother have established a special relationship. As long as he can continue to care for her by himself, they can maintain the illusion that nothing has changed.

Your mother may be willing to accept help but unwilling to oppose your father. Or she might not want to be cared for by strangers. (If this were the case, your father's refusal to accept help could arise from respect for your mother's feelings.) If it is not clear who is needing what, you may need to speak with your parents separately or listen for unspoken messages. (See page 12 for guidance on how to do this.)

4. What's hooking you?

Although there is good reason to be concerned about your parents' situation, nothing terrible has happened yet, nor is it likely to in the very near future. If you feel compelled to do something immediately, your own needs may be affecting your judgment.

You may be motivated, for example, by your strong feelings about how your parents *should* be living during their final years and by your belief that truly loving children don't allow their parents to live as your parents are living. You may be ashamed of the conditions in their home.

You may also worry about what others will think of you for allowing these conditions to continue. If a visitor commented about the dust balls on the floor or about the dirty bathroom, you would be embarrassed. If your mother's physician commented on her body odor, you would be mortified. Even though you may believe in respecting your parents' wishes, it can be difficult to explain your motives to others.

5. Who must be included in problem-solving discussions?

Since your parents will not acknowledge that a problem exists, the burden is initially on you to generate possible solutions. Once you have thought through your options, you must approach your parents and secure their consent and cooperation. If none of your ideas is acceptable, you might ask *them* to come up with something they would be willing to try.

6. What is your goal?

You want your parents to accept the help they need so they can maintain an adequate quality of life. You want to do this without threatening your father's pride or your parents' sense of autonomy.

Solve the Problem

1. Decide on the needs your solution must satisfy.

Any successful solution to your problem must guarantee that your mother is adequately cared for without overtaxing your father. The solution must satisfy both your parents, and if at all possible, avoid undermining your relationship with them. Finally, it must not ask too much of you or anyone else who may be involved.

2. Come up with a few possible solutions.

Doing nothing for the time being and taking a wait-and-see approach is one option, since the situation is not yet urgent. Finding a more active solution to your parents' problem is a challenge, since they are so invested in maintaining their independence. The most logical solution—finding competent professional help to supplement your father's caregiving—is not an option at this time because of your parents' resistance.

However, you still may be able to offer help in ways that don't threaten your parents' self-reliance. For example, you might offer to pick up some items for them at the supermarket when you do your own shopping or ask a neighbor to do the same. You might also give them as a holiday or birthday gift a certificate for a one-time-only visit from a local house-cleaning service. These are small ways to help them without broadcasting that they are losing the ability to cope. Such incremental solutions have no stigma attached, since they are actions anyone might welcome. They will allow you to get your foot in the door, to break through your parents' need to handle everything by themselves. Once you have set this new precedent, your parents might be open to more regular help.

As your parents' needs become more acute, and as they become more willing to accept help, you might be able to move on to a third possible solution: to arrange for professional help from a home health agency. When the time comes to propose this, you will almost certainly need to reassure your father that he will remain your mother's primary caregiver, and that the main purpose of their getting help is to allow them to stay in their own home without compromising their quality of life.

The least desirable and most heavy-handed solution is to demand that your parents accept help immediately, and if they refuse, to threaten to report them to state authorities charged with the responsibility of investigating claims of elder abuse and neglect. This approach—born of *your* needs, not theirs—lets them know how strongly you feel, but at the price of your relationship with them.

3. Analyze the choices and select the best solution.

(See chart on opposite page.)

Given your parents' resistance to in-home help, it is probably best to try an incremental strategy.

GOAL: How can I convince my parents to accept help?

NEEDS	POSSIBLE SOLUTIONS			
	Do nothing	Use an incremental strategy	Arrange for a home health aide	Threaten to report them to authorities
Must ensure your parents' safety and health	yes, for the time being—but not for much longer	yes, to some extent	yes	yes, provided you are prepared to follow through
Must be acceptable to your parents	yes	possibly	probably not	no
Must allow you to maintain a good relationship with your parents	yes	probably	probably not	no
Must be practical and workable	not for long	probably	probably	yes, but at the price of your relationship

4. Conduct a Murphy's Law analysis.

One problem that might arise is that your parents accept your offers of help on a limited basis, but refuse to accept them on a more regular one. Depending on what they are willing to allow, they may be no better off than they were before.

Your father might refuse to accept any help at all. If this happens, you have little choice but to wait it out, remaining vigilant for signs of impending crisis. At that point, you can appropriately intervene more aggressively with one of your other options.

A third potential problem could arise with your incremental approach if it involves people other than yourself (for example, the neighbor you ask to shop for your parents). These people can change their minds, become ill, or otherwise upset your plans. To prevent this from happening, choose your helpers carefully and be clear about what you need them to do and when they need to do it. Have backup people available, or be prepared to fill in yourself. Once you get your parents' expectations up, you don't want to disappoint them.

5. *Carry out your plan.*

Begin by acknowledging your father's hard work. Then offer help in a way that does not suggest you think he is incapable. You can say something like this: "Dad, you've been doing a wonderful job taking care of Mom. But I'm concerned that with all your time spent taking care of her, there aren't enough hours in the day for food shopping as well. If you can make a list up for me, I can take care of it next Saturday when I do my own food shopping." Or say, "Dad, I know you have your hands full taking care of Mom, and I wonder if you could use a little time for yourself. I enjoy visiting Mom and would be happy to give you a break for a few hours on Saturday, if you'd like." In both cases, you are making it easy for your father to accept help because he isn't being asked to pay for it with his pride.

If you wanted to give your father a one-time-only gift of help, you might present it by saying, "Dad, I didn't know what to get you for Father's Day (or your birthday, etc.), but I know you don't need another tie or belt. So I took the money I would have spent and got you a gift certificate to a local cleaning service for a full house cleaning. My neighbors use them all the time and are very satisfied."

By using these strategies, you are making it clear to your father that he can accept help without relinquishing his role as your mother's caregiver. Moreover, you are getting both him and your mother used to the idea of accepting help.

Once you have convinced your parents to accept some kind of help, however small, you are on the right track toward your goal of arranging for additional help. As your parents' tolerance increases, you and they should be able to talk together openly. You can listen to their objections and respond by providing necessary information and reassurance. As long as you keep in mind their need to feel in control of their lives, you will not go wrong.

6. Evaluate your progress.

You will know that you have reached your goal when your parents are accepting sufficient help to maintain adequate levels of nutrition and self-care.

↶

My parents fight like cats and dogs, and now my mother won't take care of my father.

Situation

Your mother and father have never gotten along well. As their only child, you recall that throughout your childhood they always seemed to be at odds with each other. During one cross-country trip, for example, they bickered constantly about every imaginable thing. Your mother complained about your father's driving, the motels he chose, and the foods he ate. He, in turn, faulted her for her inability to pack suitcases properly, her sleeping habits, and the clothing she wore.

Among friends and within the family, your parents have had the reputation of being at each other's throats constantly. By the time you were out of college you had had enough. You drifted away from your parents, unwilling to witness their incessant battles or play the part of referee any longer.

Unfortunately, as they have aged, nothing has changed. During your occasional, dutiful visits, you have noticed that, if anything, the situation has deteriorated. As their dependency on one another has increased, each has become more angry with and more critical of the other.

A few weeks ago you received a call from your mother. She told you that your father had had a mild heart attack, and she was caring for him now after his brief stay in the hospital. She complained that he was an awful patient and that she couldn't manage him. She asked you to come help her take care of him and said that if you couldn't, she would put him into a nursing home or rehabilitation facility. After checking with your father's doctor, you learned that your father's condition was not problematic and your mother could easily take care of him. The doctor, although aware of your parents' mutual antagonism, urged you to find a way to keep your father at home.

Last week, you arranged to stay with your parents for a short period of time to see what you could do to help them. When you arrived, you were immediately assaulted by a barrage of complaints from both of them.

Clarify the Problem

1. Does everyone agree a problem exists?

While everyone agrees there is a problem, each of you sees it differently. For your mother, the problem is your father. For your father, it is your mother. And for you, it is your worry that your mother will place your father, inappropriately, into some kind of residential facility.

2. How urgent is the problem, really?

The situation is fairly urgent for two reasons. First, your father needs to be cared for while he recovers from his heart attack. Second, your mother is unwilling to provide that care and is threatening to institutionalize him, which is a waste of both the family's and the institution's resources. Something must be done *now* to prevent that from happening.

3. What is behind your parents' problematic behaviors?

Although your parents never saw eye to eye, they managed to stay together all this time. As mature adults, they could have terminated their relationship at any time, yet they found ways to accommodate each other and chose to remain together. Your father's heart attack disrupted the status quo, and suddenly their relationship changed. Now your mother resents having to take care of someone with whom she is chronically angry, and your father hates feeling dependent.

4. What's hooking you?

The fact that you responded to your mother's distress call indicates that you care about your parents. You could have told your mother you didn't want to get involved and to handle the problem herself, but you didn't. However, now you are caught between your desire to help your parents and your anger at their inability to take care of things themselves. In addition, your mother has made *you* responsible for whether your father goes into a facility. While it is appropriate for you to help your parents find options to resolve their dilemma, you must not allow them to bully you into becoming your father's caregiver.

5. Who must be included in problem-solving discussions?

For the time being, your parents and you are the only people who should be discussing this problem. At some later point, you may want to bring in others to provide information or to offer suggestions.

6. What is your goal?

Your immediate goal is to find a way to make it possible for your mother to take care of your father without institutionalizing him. (A longer-term goal, if you can achieve it, is to help your parents find a way to get along, so they can rely on each other in the future as their health deteriorates and as their dependence on each other increases. However, accomplishing this now is not an essential element in resolving the dilemma you are currently coping with.)

Solve the Problem

1. Decide on the needs your solution must satisfy.

Your solution must provide your father with appropriate care while he recuperates. It must not foster dependency on you, and it should preserve your parents' resources. (Once again, ideally, your solution should also provide ways to help your parents cope more effectively with similar situations in the future.)

2. Come up with a few possible solutions.

Since your mother does not want to take full responsibility for your father's care, one solution is to arrange for someone to come to their home to assist her. If she wants absolutely no part of your father's care, another solution is to hire someone to provide all the in-home care. (This assumes they have the financial resources to do so.) The presence of a stranger in the house might also serve to restrain your parents' mutually antagonistic behavior.

If they do not want to have someone come into their home, and your mother refuses to provide care herself, a nursing home or rehabilitation facility is the only solution.

3. Analyze the choices and select the best solution.

(See chart on next page.)

Having both your mother and hired help provide care for your father is the preferred solution.

4. Conduct a Murphy's Law analysis.

The success of your plan depends on your parents' cooperation. Make clear to them that even if home help doesn't work out, you will not stay to take care of your father. Success also depends on the experience and interpersonal skills of the helper you hire. Since your parents are difficult to deal with, you need to find someone experienced at working with difficult people, and let him or her know the specific problems likely to be encountered.

GOAL: How can I arrange for my father to be cared for adequately?

	POSSIBLE SOLUTIONS			
NEEDS	Do nothing	Mother and hired help provide care	Hired help alone provides care	Put father into a nursing home or rehabilitation facility
Must ensure that your father gets the care he needs	no	yes	yes	yes
Must avoid fostering dependency on you	yes, provided you do not become involved in your father's care	yes	yes	yes
Must preserve family and institutional resources	yes, but for a short time only	yes, to some degree (depends on cost of home care)	yes, but cost of home care can be substantial	no

5. Carry out your plan.

First, you need to let both parents know that you came home for the sole purpose of helping them find a way to solve their problem. Emphasize that you will be with them for only a short period of time.

Next, persuade them at least to try home help. You might say something like this to your mother: "Mom, Dr. Jones assured me that Dad does not need more than home care. I know you're having a hard time caring for Dad by yourself, but it would be a waste of your money to put him into a nursing home or rehabilitation facility when it's not needed. Would you consider getting someone to come in to give you a hand taking care of him?" Take even a grudging acknowledgment as a signal to continue.

Address your father and let him know his cooperation would be required, too: "Dad, if we do hire someone to come in to help Mom, you'll need to cooperate and go along with the plan. If you do, you can manage just fine at home and get better quickly. But if you don't, you'll need to be admitted to a nursing home or a rehabilitation facility. That would not only be unnecessary, it would be inconvenient and expensive as well."

Depending on your parents' responses, you may need to offer them additional facts, such as the actual cost per day of a nursing home versus the cost of home care. You will also need to tell them what to expect if a home care worker is brought in. Reassure them that you will help them hire a competent helper and that you will be with them the day the helper arrives.

Once they agree to try home help, your task will be to find an agency capable of providing a suitable helper. (See *Choosing a Home Health Agency* on pages 86–87 for guidance on locating and screening an agency.) Given the difficulty your parents have agreeing on anything, it will make sense for you to take primary (although not sole) responsibility for finding the agency and arranging for the helper.

Plan to be present when the helper first arrives. If all goes well, within an hour or two you will see signs that a working relationship has begun to form: your parents will seem more relaxed than when the helper first arrived, and the helper will seem comfortable and will demonstrate an ability to handle your parents competently. The proof of that competence will be in the helper's ability to ask and answer questions simply and directly, give your father the care he needs, and respond professionally to any biting remarks between your parents.

Once these indicators emerge, your presence is no longer needed. Tell your parents you are going to leave, as you said you would. Leaving as soon as it is feasible forces your parents to deal directly with the helper and prevents them from turning to you instead. Offer your parents encouragement and support. Let them know you will call them later that day and at regular intervals. Reassure them you are still available should a crisis arise.

6. Evaluate your progress.

You will know your plan is working if the professional helper stays on and your mother stops threatening to put your father into a facility. You may want to keep in touch with the helper, to express appreciation and to get periodic progress reports. If the helper quits while your father is still in need of care, and your mother once again refuses to provide it, a *temporary* stay at a facility might be the best option, unless there is reason to believe another helper will be able to deal with your parents more effectively.

My brother and I disagree with our stepmother about putting our father on life support.

Situation

Your 74-year-old father has cancer. He had a heart attack two days ago while undergoing surgery to remove a large, cancerous tumor, and he is now in a coma. The doctor says your father's prognosis is very poor and that it is unlikely he will survive for long, no matter what is done for him. Nevertheless, he can be placed on life-support systems, which will prolong his life for a short while.

Since your father does not have a living will and since he did not appoint a health care proxy, your family must decide on a course of action. You and your brother are quite sure that your father would not want to be kept alive under such circumstances. Your stepmother, on the other hand, wants to keep him alive for as long as possible, by any means, and regardless of expense. Since there is no hope that your father will recover, an expenditure of perhaps tens of thousands of dollars makes no sense to you and your brother.

You both generally get along well with your stepmother and have tried to convince her to let your father die a natural death, but she will not listen. Instead, she has become angry with you and has told the doctor to disregard what you both say.

Clarify the Problem

1. Does everyone agree a problem exists?

Everyone agrees that a decision must be made about your father's care. However, your brother and you disagree with your stepmother about which course of action to take. You believe her desire to put your father on life support is contrary to your father's wishes. She believes you two are intruding on her right to determine what treatment her husband receives.

2. How urgent is the problem, really?

This problem is urgent. Your stepmother knows that if life support is to be effective, it must begin soon. However, you know that once your father is put on life support, it will be more difficult to have it removed than to have prevented its use in the first place. A decision must be made within a day or two.

3. What is behind your stepmother's problematic behavior?

Your stepmother is reacting emotionally to the impending loss of her husband. Although she understands that he will not live long, she is reluctant to make the decision that will allow him to die. In addition, as his wife, she feels that you and your brother are overstepping your bounds by trying to influence her decision.

4. What's hooking you?

You are motivated by the concern that your father's wishes be respected and by the desire that he not suffer needlessly. In addition, you and your brother may feel that because you are your father's biological family, your voices should carry more weight than your stepmother's. Someone will have to make the decision, and you don't think it should be your stepmother.

5. Who must be included in problem-solving discussions?

The decision-making power rests with all three of you, although your stepmother is the person whose opinions your father's physician will probably consider most seriously.

6. What is your goal?

You hope to convince your stepmother to join your brother and you in directing your father's physician to withhold life support. If all three of you are in agreement, the physician will be more likely to respect your wishes.

Solve the Problem

1. Decide on the needs your solution must satisfy.

The solution must satisfy your stepmother that she is making the right decision, allowing her to put aside her misgivings and be confident that this is what your father would prefer. In doing so, the solution must be sensitive to your stepmother's feelings.

Finally, the solution must satisfy you and your brother that you are doing all you can to ensure that your father gets the care he would want.

2. Come up with a few possible solutions.

In order to persuade your stepmother to join the two of you in directing your father's physician to forego life support, you need to demonstrate that this is what your father would want. One solution, therefore, is to provide direct evidence of his wishes—perhaps in the form of a letter. If nothing like that exists, you might convince your stepmother by recalling conversations in which your father commented negatively about a friend or relative who was kept alive by life support and suffered as a result. Alternatively, if you cannot offer definitive proof of your father's wishes, you might infer what he *probably* would want, given his personality and attitude toward life.

Another approach is to inform your stepmother of what will happen if your father is placed on life support. This can be done through literature from a "Right to Die" organization, which spells out what life support really means. You might also arrange for her to speak with a critical care nurse, or someone else with firsthand knowledge and experience, who can describe a feeding tube, a respirator, and other devices used to sustain life. Once the concept of life support is presented realistically, she might very well change her mind. (See *The Right to Die* on opposite page.)

3. Analyze the choices and select the best solution.

GOAL: How can we convince our stepmother to tell our father's physician to withhold life support?

	POSSIBLE SOLUTIONS		
NEEDS	Do nothing	Convince your stepmother that you know your father's wishes	Tell your stepmother what will happen to your father if he is put on life support
Must satisfy your stepmother that she is making the right choice	no	possibly	possibly
Must be sensitive to your stepmother's emotional needs	yes	yes, if you are tactful	yes, if you are gentle
Must satisfy you and your brother that you are doing all you can to ensure that your father's wishes are respected	no	yes	yes

Given your stepmother's resistance, the preferred solution is a combination of logical arguments that demonstrate you know what your father would want and information about what life support involves.

4. Conduct a Murphy's Law analysis.

Your stepmother may refuse to listen to anything you say regarding your father's wishes or information about life support. If she

The Right to Die

In 1991 Congress responded to widespread concern over the use of artificial devices to maintain life at outrageous cost and at the expense of personal dignity. It passed the Patient Self-Determination Act, which guarantees the right of every person to control which medical procedures are employed at the time of death. Advance directives (the living will, the health care proxy, the durable power of attorney for health care, and medical directives) are the means by which a person can make his or her wishes known.

Unfortunately, advance directives are not always respected. The most common reason for this is that many errors are made in preparing them, including the following:

- failure to provide specific information in a directive;

- improper witnesses (for example, a living will cannot be legally witnessed by a family member or by any other person having an interest in the estate of the dying person);

- failure to establish that the person completing a directive understood what the document meant and took enough time to decide what he or she wanted (in other words, gave "informed consent").

Information about advance directives can be obtained from a number of organizations and on the Internet. If more help is needed, an elder law attorney can be consulted. However, an attorney is seldom necessary, and some do take advantage of people in distress by charging exorbitant fees. Shop around. Read.

The resources listed on the next page will get you started on your research into advance directives.

continued on next page

The Right to Die—*continued*

- Enter the phrase "Right to Die" in any Internet search engine. This will yield Web sites and other sources of information. One of the most interesting is www .uslivingwillregistry.com, a free service providing information, forms, and a national registry service.

- Members of the **NATIONAL ACADEMY OF ELDER LAW ATTORNEYS** have a special interest in elder law matters. For a list of members in your area, write the organization at 1604 North Country Club Road, Tucson, AZ 85716, or contact them at (520) 881-4005 or www.naela.com/.

---

is completely closed-minded, you have no choice but to try to convince your father's physician that you and your brother, not your stepmother, know what your father would want.

Even if your stepmother is willing to listen, there is no guarantee that your arguments will persuade her. If that is the case, you might ask what *would* convince her, and try to collect the evidence needed.

Another way of gauging what might persuade her is to observe her reactions to your arguments and then modify your approach. For example, if she responds more favorably to anecdotes that present your father as someone who would not want life support than she does to logical arguments, then use as many anecdotes as possible.

5. Carry out your plan.

If there is any chance you are going to succeed in having a discussion about this emotionally charged topic, you need to pay special attention to four crucial factors: the time and place you talk, the tone you set, the sensitivity with which you prepare your case, and the actual arguments you use.

As soon as you can, find a time and place where you, your

brother, and your stepmother can talk meaningfully and calmly. The hospital, with all its unfamiliar sights, sounds, and smells, is probably not the place to try. If possible, look for a private, quiet, and neutral setting.

Set a tone of calmness and deliberation. Even though you hope to persuade your stepmother to see things your way, you should approach the discussion as an exploration of issues and a search for the best course of action. If possible, avoid having your talk degenerate into a debate or an argument. Do this by laying out the issues systematically and offering information in an objective way. "We're here to decide what Dad would want if he were able to tell us," you might say. "We can't know for sure, but we can look back on things he said and the kinds of choices he made about other things, and maybe get some guidance from that."

In planning what you will say, make a special effort to be sensitive to what your stepmother is likely feeling, especially her concern that you and your brother are trying to usurp her rights. Make it very clear that all three of you have your father's best interests at heart and that the nature of your ties with him— whether as his biological family or as his wife—is less critical than making sure he is treated as he would want to be.

Listen more than you talk. Try to find out the basis for your stepmother's wanting to put your father on life support. The more you know about her reasons, the more likely you are to respond sensitively. For example, if you know she is terrified at the thought of letting him die, give her an opportunity to talk about her fear. Unless you allow her that, she will never be able to approach the problem rationally. Once she *is* able to, offer arguments tailored to her special concerns. You might say something like, "I know the idea of letting Dad die is awful. None of us wants to lose him. But if the alternative is to stick tubes into his body, rob him of any dignity, and allow him to linger in agony, the choice isn't quite so hard."

6. Evaluate your progress.

You will have succeeded if your stepmother agrees to join you and your brother in directing your father's doctor to withhold life support.

❧

My mother is going to a doctor I think is a quack, but she refuses to stop seeing him.

Situation

Your mother is 77 years old. When she was diagnosed with a slow-growing, malignant tumor a year ago, her oncologist recommended a course of radiation and chemotherapy. She declined. "I know too many people who have gone through that," she said, "and the treatment was worse than the disease. Not me!" Instead, she began reading health magazines. Soon she was looking into cancer "cures" that rely on nutritional supplements and other unproven treatments.

On the recommendation of the owner of her local health food store, she got to know a physician who practices alternative medicine and who promised her a cure. For the past year, he has been providing treatment that you believe is quackery. He has been giving her massive doses of vitamins and minerals, and applying magnets to the site of her tumor. She has already spent over ten thousand dollars—none of it reimbursable by her health insurance.

Soon after you learned what was involved in your mother's alternative treatments, you spoke with your mother's internist as well as her oncologist about your concern. Both were dismayed. You tried talking with your mother, gently suggesting that she get a second opinion. However, she insisted that her new doctor could cure her. In addition, she said that he was "a very nice man" and she didn't want to hurt his feelings. Now, a year later, there are no signs that your mother is getting better. If anything, she seems worse.

Clarify the Problem

1. Does everyone agree a problem exists?

Your mother is quite satisfied with her treatment, or at least she seems to be. You, her internist, and her oncologist, however, believe that her treatment is inappropriate and the situation serious.

2. How urgent is the problem, really?

The problem is urgent. Unless your mother's cancer has gone into remission, she may reach a point beyond which she cannot be helped at all. Moreover, she is spending huge sums of money on treatment and supplements that you fear may only be lining the pockets of the physician and the health food store owner.

3. What is behind your mother's problematic behavior?

Fear certainly is a factor. The diagnosis of cancer is terrifying, and the prospect of radiation and chemotherapy is equally awful. It is little wonder your mother is grasping at any alternative that gives her hope.

Having begun this course of treatment, whether or not it is effective, your mother may feel embarrassed at the prospect of admitting she might have been wrong. Hence, the longer she receives the treatment, the more committed she is likely to become.

Her unwillingness to hurt or offend her present physician may also discourage her from taking steps to protect herself.

4. What's hooking you?

Real concerns for your mother's health and welfare are fueling your distress. However, it is also likely you are upset with her for

174

being so easily persuaded, and furious with the health food store owner and the treating physician who may be exploiting her. Unless you keep these feelings in check, your attempts to resolve this dilemma by convincing her to reconsider her decision will most likely deteriorate into futile and angry accusations.

5. Who must be included in problem-solving discussions?

Since no one but your mother has the authority to make the ultimate decision about the kind of treatment she receives, any discussions will involve just the two of you.

6. What is your goal?

You want to know whether your mother's current treatment is working. If it isn't, you want her to undertake a recognized course of therapy.

Solve the Problem

1. Decide on the needs your solution must satisfy.

Your solution must allow you to find out whether your mother's treatment is having any effect. If it is, there is no reason to push her to change. If it is not, you will have a logical basis for urging her to reconsider her decision. The solution must also make it possible for your mother to change her mind without feeling foolish and without offending her physician. Finally, your solution must help lessen your mother's fear of conventional treatment to the degree that she can consider it seriously.

2. Come up with a few possible solutions.

One solution is to convince your mother to undergo tests that compare the current state of her tumor with its status a year ago. You agree that if her condition has improved, you will leave her alone and let her continue her present course of treatment. She agrees that if the results show no improvement, she will abandon her current treatment and undergo conventional radiation and chemotherapy.

Another possible solution is to have your mother undergo the tests but without requiring any promises of future action on her part. This solution, although weaker than the first, will be less frightening for her and will let you know whether her current treatment is working.

A third possibility is to have her join a cancer support group, with the hope that contact with people who have actually undergone radiation and chemotherapy will lessen her fears.

3. Analyze the choices and select the best solution.

(See chart on opposite page.)

The preferred solution is to convince your mother to agree to undergo conventional treatment if the results of testing indicate her treatment is not helping.

4. Conduct a Murphy's Law analysis.

Your mother may refuse to commit herself to your proposal for fear that the news will be bad and she will have to leave the comfort of a familiar physician. If this happens, use your second solution as a fallback position: try to get her to agree to testing anyway, with no further commitment required on her part. Although less desirable, this will let you know her medical status and will give her a reason to change her mind, should she be ready.

Even if your mother agrees initially to undergo radiation and chemotherapy should the results indicate they are needed, she may change her mind and insist on staying with her current treatment. If it turns out that fear of the unknown is at the heart of her opposition, you might address this fear by getting her information about the proposed treatment, having her speak with medical personnel and technicians who administer it, or suggesting she attend a cancer support group.

5. Carry out your plan.

Before speaking with your mother, find out what kind of testing is required. You may be able to allay *some* of her anxiety by let-

GOAL: How can I be sure my mother is getting the proper treatment?

NEEDS	POSSIBLE SOLUTIONS			
	Do nothing	Convince your mother to undergo testing and, if the current treatment is not working, to agree to undergo conventional treatment	Convince your mother to undergo testing for the purpose of a status evaluation only	Convince your mother to join a cancer support group
Must tell you if your mother's current treatment is working	no	yes	yes	no
Must allow your mother to change her mind without losing face or offending her present physician	yes	yes, if her present physician is asked to participate in interpreting the results	yes, if her present physician is asked to participate in interpreting the results	yes
Must help lessen your mother's fear of conventional treatment so that she can consider it seriously	no	possibly	possibly	probably

ting her know in advance what she is agreeing to. Then speak with her and let her know why you are worried. You might say something like, "Mom, I've avoided saying anything about your cancer treatment, since I know you think highly of Dr. ____. But it's been a year now, and you don't seem to be getting better. I'd feel more comfortable if I knew for sure what was happening with your tumor. If it's getting worse, I'd like you to consider a more conventional type of treatment." You can then tell her what kind of testing she will need to undergo and try to secure her agreement. If she has misgivings about hurting her doctor's feelings, you can suggest that he participate in the interpretation of results. Reassure her that if he truly believes in the treatment he is providing, he won't be afraid to have its results evaluated. Even if your mother refuses initially to commit herself to changing anything as a result of the test findings, she may change her mind once the results are available.

6. Evaluate your progress.

If your mother is willing to undergo testing, you have passed your first milestone. Where you go from there depends on the test results. If her treatment seems to be working, and she has no desire to change, you must honor your end of the agreement. If the treatment has been ineffective, and she is willing to begin more conventional treatment, you will have reached your goal.

ॐ

My father's public behavior embarrasses me.

Situation

Your father has been tactless and opinionated for as long as you can remember, never thinking twice about commenting loudly— whatever the circumstances—on anything that is on his mind. When you were a child, you didn't realize your father's habit was unusual. However, as you moved into adolescence, then adulthood, you became acutely aware of the looks that people gave each other after your father went into one of his inappropriate commentaries. Your mother often begged him to keep his voice down, but he would rebuff her, saying that a man had a right to his opinion.

Over the years, your father's mind has remained sharp, but his hearing has worsened. As a result, his comments, as tactless and inappropriate as ever, have gotten louder. He says anything that crosses his mind, talking loudly about such things as his prostate problem and his annoyances with your mother's behavior. When this occurs your mother just raises her eyebrows and stares off into space. She has long since given up trying to quiet him and has resigned herself to the inevitable shrinking of their social circle.

Although you live nearby and see your parents often, you

now feel like avoiding every situation where you will be with your father in public.

Clarify the Problem

1. Does everyone agree a problem exists?

Everyone but your father feels that a problem exists. His behavior is not only thoroughly disagreeable, but it is causing your parents to become increasingly isolated. Your mother is embarrassed, despairing, and lonely. You hate going anywhere with your father, but you don't want to punish your mother by staying away.

2. How urgent is the problem, really?

Your father has been behaving this way for years; considered in *that* sense, the situation is not urgent. However, the deterioration of his hearing makes it likely that his behavior will become even more intolerable. And your mother's increasing isolation may already have put her at risk for depression. Therefore, you probably should act as soon as you have a workable plan.

3. What is behind your father's problematic behavior?

At this point in your father's life, his personality traits are deeply ingrained and difficult to change. The situation has worsened as a function of his declining hearing. He is apparently unaware that his voice is carrying quite so much and that other people are acutely aware of what he is saying. In addition, his contentiousness is fueled by disagreement. The more you shush him, the louder and more obnoxious he becomes.

4. What's hooking you?

Since children, even grown ones, are identified with their parents, it is not surprising that you are embarrassed by your father's loud and obnoxious behavior. If he were someone else's father, you might be more tolerant, perhaps even amused. But it is painful to watch people cringe when it is *your* father they are responding to. You are also concerned for your mother's well-being, and you fear that her loneliness will lead to depression.

5. Who must be included in problem-solving discussions?

There are only three people involved here: your father, your mother, and you. Since your father does not see his conduct as a problem, and your mother long ago gave up trying to change him, it is up to you to find a way to curb his behavior.

6. What is your goal?

You are hoping to keep your father from carrying on as loudly and as frequently as he has been. You know that you can't alter his basic nature, but you and your mother may be able to affect his behavior. Your goal is to be able to appear in public with him without wishing you were somewhere else.

Solve the Problem

1. Decide on the needs your solution must satisfy.

Your solution must satisfy both your mother's and your need to be able to be with your father in public without cringing every time he opens his mouth. In more specific terms, you want your father to speak more softly and make fewer offensive remarks.

2. Come up with a few possible solutions.

Because of his hearing loss, your father is speaking more loudly. You can do a couple of things in this regard. First, you can point it out to him each time he does it and ask him to speak more softly.

Second, you can suggest that he get fitted for a hearing aid, so that he will realize when he is talking too loudly. This won't make his outbursts any less obnoxious, but at least it may soften their impact.

Third, because you know that pleading with your father to moderate his ill-tempered remarks is likely to be futile, you might try a new strategy. *Avoid* arguing with him. Instead, empathize, if you can. Agreeing with him, or even just nodding, can take the wind out of his sails.

For example, suppose you've taken your father out to a fine restaurant. All is going well until he tries to butter his bread and finds the butter too cold to spread. He starts complaining loudly about how he hates cold butter and how stupid the waiters are to serve it. Resist the urge to say, "Dad, please quiet down. It's not worth making a fuss over." This will only annoy him and possibly fuel his anger. Instead, agree with him and propose that you ask the waiter to warm the butter in the microwave. What can your father say then? In fact, he may surprise you and say he can manage.

It may be difficult to validate your father's feelings when they seem irrational, especially when you are angered or embarrassed by them and by their expression, but these are the times when validation is needed most. So the next time your father carries on—whether about cold butter or the price of a movie ticket—agree with him. You may get lucky and buy some peace.

A final, if somewhat drastic, option is to see your parents only in the privacy of their home. By doing this, you can spare yourself grief but still stay in touch. You don't want to punish your mother for your father's behavior, so seeing them at home will at least allow you to visit your mother. You can let your parents know that you will cut short your visit if your father becomes unpleasant or abusive.

3. Analyze the choices and select the best solution.

(See chart on opposite page.)

A combined solution—getting your father a hearing aid and validating his feelings—is your best bet. The last option, visiting your parents only in their home, does not address the issue of your father's public behavior or your mother's needs, but it does allow you to continue seeing them without subjecting yourself to public humiliation and abuse.

GOAL: How can I be with my father in public without him embarrassing me?

NEEDS	POSSIBLE SOLUTIONS			
	Do nothing	Get your father a hearing aid	Validate your father's feelings	Limit contact with your parents to their home
Must result in your father talking more softly in public	no	probably	no	no
Must result in fewer offensive and critical remarks	no	unlikely	possibly	possibly
Must allow you and your mother to be with your father in public without great embarrassment	no	possibly	possibly	no

4. Conduct a Murphy's Law analysis.

Your father may not be willing to be fitted for a hearing aid, and even if he gets one, he may refuse to wear it. (See dilemma 13 on pages 131–136 for help with this particular problem.) You should anticipate these possibilities and speak with an audiologist prior to bringing your father in for testing. An experienced audiologist will be familiar with your concerns and may be able to convince your father to try a hearing aid.

The second part of the solution, to empathize with your father or validate his feelings, is more easily said than done. If you are too angry or embarrassed, nothing you say will come out right. To get the necessary distance from your feelings, try treating the situation as a game in which you *must* agree with whatever your father says. It is artificial and contrived, but it may be just what you need to get the process going, provided your manner is neither smug nor condescending.

If you elect not to be with your parents in public, your

father may become angry with you. Tell him that you are doing this only as a last resort, and that if he agrees to control his behavior, you will gladly resume seeing them elsewhere. If he values your company or considers your mother's well-being, this may give him an incentive to watch his words.

You might also want to keep tabs on your mother's emotional well-being. If you become concerned, you can offer to arrange for her to see a therapist. Be aware, however, that she has lived with your father for a long time and may not be open to change.

5. Carry out your plan.

Lay the appropriate groundwork before trying to have your father fitted with a hearing aid. (See *Hearing Loss and Treatment* on page 135.) Enlist the support of his physician, especially if they have a good relationship. Speak in advance with the audiologist for advice on how to prepare your father for what will happen and how to deal with his concerns. When you have obtained your father's agreement, arrange for the hearing test and fitting.

Let your mother know about your plans to validate your father's feelings and why you think it may work, and solicit her cooperation. Having an ally for yourself will make it easier for you to carry out your plan.

6. Evaluate your progress.

You will know soon enough whether your solutions are working. If you are able to change your father's behavior just enough to make being with him tolerable and to give your mother more of a social life, then you are well on the way to meeting your goal. As a by-product, you may even end up having a better relationship with both parents than you have had in the past.

༄

My mother is no longer stable on her feet, but she insists on climbing on chairs to reach her cabinets.

Situation

Your mother's height has often made her the target of affectionate teasing. At 4'11", she is by far the tiniest member of your family. As a younger woman and homemaker she often compensated for her lack of height by climbing on chairs rather than asking for help to reach items in her cabinets, especially in the kitchen.

She has aged now—she is approaching 90—and has remained fiercely independent. This spirit of self-reliance generally serves her well. However, in her determination to maintain her autonomy, she continues to climb on chairs to reach items she needs. This troubles you because she is no longer as stable on her feet as she once was, and an injury at this stage of her life could have far-reaching repercussions. Moreover, she lives alone, and you worry that if something were to happen to her, there would be no one there to help. You have spoken with her about your concern, but she minimizes it and reassures you she is perfectly safe—after all, she has been climbing on chairs for years. You dread her falling, not only because of the consequences for her, but for you, as well. Despite her reassurances, you live in a state of constant fear.

Clarify the Problem

1. Does everyone agree a problem exists?

Not only does your mother not agree a problem exists, she would be furious if you tried to limit her right to do whatever she wants. You, alone, think this a serious problem and are concerned about her behavior.

2. How urgent is the problem, really?

Your mother hasn't fallen yet. Nevertheless, her continued climbing represents an accident waiting to happen. For her sake and yours, you can't look the other way any longer. The sooner this problem is addressed and resolved, the better for both of you.

3. What is behind your mother's problematic behavior?

Your mother's independence and self-sufficiency are crucial parts of her self-image. If she stops climbing on chairs, she will no longer be able to manage around her own kitchen, the heart of her home, without asking for help. And by no longer continuing to do what she has done all her life, she will be forced to acknowledge her limitations. It's little wonder that she has an emotional investment in *not* changing.

4. What's hooking you?

You are understandably afraid that your mother will hurt herself. A broken hip at her age can become a permanent handicap, which would be tragic for her and would increase your responsibilities tremendously.

You may also fear that you will be blamed if you let something happen to her. You can imagine people saying, "What kind of person would allow her 90-year-old mother to climb on chairs?"

5. Who must be included in problem-solving discussions?

It is up to you to work this out with your mother.

6. What is your goal?

You would like your mother to stop climbing. If that is not possible, you would like to make it safer for her to climb and provide her with a way to summon help if she falls.

Solve the Problem

1. Decide on the needs your solution must satisfy.

Your solution must reduce as much as possible the risks associated with your mother's climbing. You also want to ensure her self-sufficiency, which is directly linked to her self-esteem. Finally, you want her to be able to summon help in case of an emergency.

2. Come up with a few possible solutions.

You cannot stop your mother from climbing on chairs if she wants to. One option, therefore, is to reduce her *need* to climb by offering to rearrange her kitchen so that the things she needs are within easy reach. You can also add more floor-level storage space, such as a free-standing cabinet.

If her kitchen is set up so that she absolutely cannot avoid climbing, you can at least get a safe and stable step stool with railings to help her keep her balance. (See *Step Stools and Adaptive Devices* on page 189.)

In addition, you can arrange for an emergency personal response system to enable your mother to summon help in the event she falls and cannot reach a phone. (See *Emergency Personal Response Systems* on page 190.)

3. Analyze the choices and select the best solution.

(See chart on next page.)

The safest and preferred solution is to offer to rearrange your mother's kitchen to eliminate her need to climb.

GOAL: How can I reduce the danger that results from my mother's climbing?

NEEDS	POSSIBLE SOLUTIONS			
	Do nothing	Offer to rearrange her kitchen so she can reach things without climbing	Buy her a step stool with rails	Offer to arrange for an emergency personal response system
Must reduce the risks associated with her climbing	no	yes	yes	yes, but only *after* an accident has occurred
Must help her to remain independent	yes, but not indefinitely	yes	yes	yes
Must enable her to summon help in the event of a fall	no	n/a	n/a	yes

4. Conduct a Murphy's Law analysis.

Your mother might not welcome your offer to rearrange her kitchen, maintaining that it works fine for her the way it is. She will probably be more willing to agree if she is given a voice in the changes to be made, and if she is encouraged to help select any free-standing cabinets or storage pieces. If she is especially stubborn, ask her to try the new arrangement, allowing that you can always put things back the way they were.

If she insists on keeping her kitchen the way it is or restores items to their original places after you have relocated them, you have little choice but to get her a step stool with rails and an emergency personal response system. While you cannot be certain that she will use the stool or wear her personal response activator, the very act of providing them will impress on her the seriousness of the dangers associated with her climbing.

5. Carry out your plan.

Since your mother sees no problem with her climbing on chairs and assures you that she is perfectly safe, your first step must be

Step Stools and Adaptive Devices

Using the phrase "step stool" in an Internet search engine, you can learn about various models of step stools. Major manufacturers, such as Cosco and Samsonite, make step stools with top rails for safety. You can also check with your local hardware store, discount store, or warehouse club.

Especially safe step stools with one or two side rails are available by mail from RONCO SALES ORGANISATION. Although expensive, they are far cheaper than medical costs if your mother falls. You can view these step stools, which come in a variety of colors and styles and are easy to move around, at www.ronco.co.uk.

For information on related products and other adaptive devices that make life safer and more comfortable, go to www.comforthouse.com/.

to convince her that your concern is legitimate. Talk with her about the consequences of falls at her age. Remind her that no one, no matter how careful, is immune.

Strategies for persuading her to try your plan might include the following:

- Ask her to consider making changes for *your* peace of mind.

- Make it clear that if she goes along with your ideas, she will still be able to do everything she is currently doing, but with less risk.

- Be specific about what kinds of changes you are considering. They may be less disruptive than she imagines.

Once you have convinced your mother and she agrees to give your plan a try, talk with her about her needs and preferences. Ask her which items she uses frequently and which she must climb on a chair to reach. Observe her as she works around

Emergency Personal Response Systems

These systems are made up of an activation device—usually a pendant or wrist band—and a base unit similar to a speaker phone that is hooked up to your parent's phone. If your parent falls or another emergency arises, she can press the button on the pendant or wrist band. This will activate her phone to call an operator available 24 hours a day through the vendor you have chosen. The operator will call back immediately and establish what help is needed. The operator, who will have access to your parent's emergency numbers, such as police, fire, ambulance, and physician, will summon help and notify the nearest neighbor or relative. If your parent cannot communicate with the operator for whatever reason, the operator will summon help immediately.

Emergency personal response systems are available through private vendors. There is a set-up charge and a monthly fee. Using an Internet search engine and the phrase "emergency personal response systems" will yield scores of companies. Compare their prices. You can also contact your state's Office of the Aging or Social Services Department for information about eligibility for a free system. Depending on your parent's assets and income, the set-up charge and monthly fees can be paid for by your state's Medicaid program.

the kitchen. Invite her to suggest ways her kitchen might be made more convenient. When you have identified the changes that need to be made (for example, she and you decide that the serving platters should be relocated), discuss the various options. Will it be sufficient to rearrange the existing cabinets? Or is additional floor-level storage needed? If additional storage is needed, find out what kind of cabinets are available. Come back to her with some choices, and let her pick what she likes.

6. Evaluate your progress.

You will know you have succeeded when your mother stops climbing on chairs. If she *does* continue to climb, your best option is to find a safer way for her to do so.

My mother moved in with us, and it's not working.

Situation

When your father died two years ago after a long illness, your mother chose to stay in the apartment they had lived in for years. She had many friends in the high-rise building, and she was active in her temple and her senior center. What's more, she seemed to adjust well to your father's passing; it was, after all, expected. As her only child, you were pleased about her decision and lent your support by arranging for a weekly house cleaner and inviting her to your home a few times a month.

For a while, she coped well. However, after several months, things began to change. Two of your mother's best friends moved to Florida. A third friend became seriously ill, and her family arranged for her to be admitted to a nursing home. Then a number of apartments in your mother's building changed hands, and the new neighbors were young and noisy. For the first time, your mother told you that she missed your father more than she expected to and that she didn't like living in her apartment anymore.

At about that same time, she began skipping meetings at her senior center and resigned her position as chairwoman of her temple's Social Committee. Your mother's rabbi called to tell you that he could not get her to change her mind and that he was concerned about her. You watched with dismay as your once-active mother continued to withdraw from others. The only time she seemed like her old self was when she visited you and your family.

After a few months of watching this decline, your husband and you decided to ask your mother to move in with you. First, you spoke with your two daughters, ages 14 and 18. They had always been close to Grandma Susan and were all for the idea. When you and your family proposed the idea to your mother, she was reluctant, fearing she would be intruding. All of you prevailed on her, however, and she eventually agreed.

You planned carefully before she arrived. Your daughters willingly agreed to share a bedroom so that Grandma could have a room of her own. Your husband and you helped your mother donate and sell off most of her possessions, except for her bedroom set and a few personal items she wanted to bring with her. In sum, you did all you could to ease her transition and to welcome her into your home.

That was six months ago. Within weeks of her arrival, your mother's behavior began to change, and within a short time she had become a terror. She started reprimanding your children, whose youthful exuberance bothered her. She also began telling you how to run your home and insulting your husband. Your family tried to understand but quickly lost patience with her. Your children started talking back to their grandmother and telling you they wanted her to leave. Your husband lost his temper once and told your mother to watch her tongue. In private he told you angrily that he never realized what a "nasty old lady" your mother was.

After insisting your mother move in with you, the thought of telling her she can't stay upsets you. But something has to change.

Clarify the Problem

1. Does everyone agree a problem exists?

Everyone but your mother has clearly said that a problem exists. You are not certain what your mother's feelings are. She hasn't said anything is wrong, but her behavior suggests otherwise.

2. How urgent is the problem, really?

The situation is urgent. Everyone is miserable, and your husband and children are losing patience. If the problem continues much longer, there could be a blow up. Your worst fears—angry outbursts, rudeness, and recriminations—may become a reality. You must act soon.

3. What is behind your mother's problematic behavior?

Your mother has become a cranky, unpleasant, and unappreciative woman. However, if that were her normal way of acting, you wouldn't have asked her to move in. There has to be more going on; this just isn't like her. Although you don't have a clear explanation for her behavior, you can make some educated guesses.

She may be upset by a clear-cut problem that she has been unable to talk about. For example, she may really dislike some aspect of her living arrangements but feel petty complaining about it, or she may regret having given away or sold off possessions that mattered to her more than she realized.

Another possibility is that she is struggling with depression. Remember, your mother was not doing well when she moved in with you. She had already begun behaving in uncharacteristic ways, such as withdrawing from her seniors group and resigning as chair of the Social Committee in her temple. She had sustained a number of losses—her friends moving away, for example—in addition to the death of your father. In all likelihood, she felt the loss of your father even more keenly after moving out of the apartment they had shared for so long. For her, moving into your home may have marked the end of one phase of her life and the beginning of another.

Finally, you may be seeing the onset of dementia. Behavior changes are not uncommon among people struggling with the loss of their capacities. Moreover, people with dementia can conceal their lapses during casual visits and appear quite normal. You would have been unaware that anything was seriously wrong with your mother until now.

4. What's hooking you?

You very likely have mixed feelings about the way your mother is acting. On the one hand, you are almost certainly angry, regardless of the reasons for her behavior. You and your family have put yourselves out. You have done more than many families would be willing to do. And in return you have received grief, rudeness, and self-centeredness.

On the other hand, you are probably concerned about these changes that you didn't anticipate and don't understand, and you are afraid of what they might mean. In addition, you may feel guilty because this is *your* mother who is making your family miserable. Even though everyone agreed to her moving in, you probably still feel responsible for the disruption she is causing.

5. Who must be included in problem-solving discussions?

You, your mother, and your husband *must* be involved in solving this problem. Your children *should* be involved, since they are affected by your decisions. If not, at the very least they should be kept informed about the steps you are taking to improve the situation.

6. What is your goal?

You want to find out what is behind your mother's behavior so that you can help her stop acting in ways that are disruptive to your family and so that she can continue to live with you.

Solve the Problem

1. Decide on the needs your solution must satisfy.

Your solution must satisfy both your family's and your need to live as you want, without being harassed by Grandma Susan. You must also be satisfied that you have made every effort to understand your mother's behavior. Finally, your solution must help remedy whatever is causing her behavior.

2. Come up with a few possible solutions.

You need to understand what is happening. The easiest way to find this out is to speak directly with your mother to ask what is bothering her. If she is aware of the reasons for her distress, your giving her the opportunity to air them may be all she really needs.

If your mother cannot tell you what is behind her behavior, you can arrange for her to see her personal physician to determine whether some medical condition is at the root of her distress.

If an apparently unresolvable family problem comes to light, you, your mother, and your family might enlist the help of a therapist familiar with eldercare issues.

If your mother is able but unwilling to do anything to improve the situation, you have no choice but to help her make other living arrangements.

3. Analyze your choices and select the best solution.

(See chart on opposite page.)

Speaking with your mother about what is troubling her is the best solution.

4. Conduct a Murphy's Law analysis.

Even if your mother knows what is bothering her and is willing to talk about it, you still may not be able to make things better. For example, if she regrets having sold off personal items that she now realizes mean a great deal to her, or if she regrets having given up her apartment, you can't do much about that. However, just getting her sadness out into the open may relieve some of her distress as well as the tension she is creating for your family.

If, when you talk with her, your mother denies that anything is troubling her, if she cannot pinpoint the source of her distress, or if a seemingly unsolvable problem is revealed, you will need to consider two of your other options, each involving outside help.

One possibility is to have your mother make an appointment with her physician to see if the source of her objectionable

GOAL: How can I get my mother to stop antagonizing my family?

NEEDS	POSSIBLE SOLUTIONS				
	Do nothing	Ask your mother to tell you what is bothering her	Have your mother see her physician for an evaluation	Arrange to see a family therapist familiar with eldercare issues	Help your mother make other living arrangements
Must satisfy your family's need to live as you want, without harassment from your mother	no	yes, once her concerns are out in the open	possibly, depending on the findings	possibly	probably
Must satisfy you that you have made an effort to understand your mother's behavior	no	yes	yes	yes	no, but this may be your only recourse
Must help resolve whatever is causing your mother's behavior	no	yes, once her concerns are out in the open	possibly	possibly	no, but this may be your only recourse

behavior can be uncovered. A skilled physician will be able to determine whether she is suffering from depression or another treatable condition. If the problem is medical rather than situational, you may not be able to solve it as readily, or—in the case of dementia—at all. However, medication may alleviate her symptoms. With information and outside help, you and your family may be able to adjust to this new situation.

If your mother's behavior stems from a problem she is encountering living in your home, a meeting with a family therapist may be able to clear up matters. Like the physician, a skilled therapist may be able to shed light on what is happening. If seeking help from a therapist is approached as a family matter, your mother may be more willing to participate than if the situation is presented as her problem alone.

Finally, if your mother is able but unwilling to do anything to make things better, she needs to understand that she cannot continue to live with you. In that case, you must help her to make other living arrangements.

5. Carry out your plan.

You must let your mother know how upset you and your family are. You can do so by saying something like this: "Mom, we're having a problem. The children and Bob are very upset with you, and I am, too. We've tried our best to welcome you, and we all looked forward to your coming. But ever since you moved in, you've been behaving in ways that are just not like you. We're concerned, and we need to know if something is bothering you." Give her specific examples of the kinds of things she has been doing, and point out their effects. Be very clear that you really want to understand what is happening. Hopefully, your mother will be receptive and will be able to talk with you about her feelings. Your job at this point is simply to listen and try to see things from her perspective. If she needs time to let your comments sink in and to gather her thoughts, arrange to speak again later.

If your mother identifies legitimate complaints having to do with the way you and the family are treating her—perhaps she thinks your daughters are being inconsiderate, for example— then arrange for everyone in the family to meet to discuss her concerns. In preparation for the meeting, ask your mother to keep track of whatever has been annoying her. You and your family should do the same. During the course of one or more meetings, work together to solve the problems that have been identified. The very act of working together may help her feel like a part of the family. (See *Family Meetings* on pages 65–66 for more information.)

If feelings run too strong, and you don't think your family can handle these meetings by yourselves, consider enlisting the help of a therapist familiar with eldercare issues to help you resolve the problem.

Again, if your mother does not know why she is feeling or behaving as she is, you need to seek the help of a professional.

6. Evaluate your progress.

It is unrealistic to think that your mother will change overnight, even if she and everyone else understands what the problems are. However, if she begins to complain less, if the tension level at home drops, and if your family's complaints become less frequent, you will know you have succeeded.

DILEMMA TWENTY-THREE

乄

My sister is stealing
from our mother.

Situation

More than a year ago your 87-year-old mother suffered a stroke, which left her virtually bedridden. She leaves the bed only to go to the bathroom and to eat her meals at a small table in her room. Your older sister, Sherry, spends almost 40 hours a week taking care of her. She also oversees a home health aide, who comes in four days a week, for a few hours each day.

You live two hours away and have two small children, so you are simply not able to be on site as often as Sherry. Even though you help out when you can, your help is limited to one or two visits a month, during which you shop and do housework.

You and your sister get along well, and until recently, everything seemed to be going fine. However, about two months ago, something odd happened while you and Sherry were talking about nursing homes. There had been a growing awareness in both your minds that primary responsibility for your mother's care would need to be turned over to professionals in the near future. Since your mother is not wealthy, the two of you began proposing ways to raise the needed money. You suggested a tag sale to sell many of the possessions your mother no longer needs, such as silverware, jewelry, paintings, and furniture. You volunteered to assume responsibility for planning the sale. To your surprise, Sherry was less than enthusiastic. She objected to every date you suggested and balked at the idea of creating an inventory of your mother's possessions. Initially, you thought she was just saddened by the prospect of seeing your mother's home broken up. However, as her objections continued, you began to wonder what was going on.

A few weekends ago, while you were visiting your mother, Sherry stepped out for an hour. Without really knowing why you were doing it, you began looking through some of your mother's things. To your dismay, you were unable to find a number of items you knew were valuable. An antique vase was missing from its usual place on the table in the hall. A gold necklace of your mother's was not in her jewelry box. A small nineteenth-century still life your father bought in Paris was not on display in the dining room. Your initial reaction was that Sherry would know where these pieces were. But when she returned and you asked, she talked in circles and gave answers that didn't make much sense.

Troubled, and feeling guilty for suspecting your sister, you began checking for other items during your next few visits. You discovered that almost all your mother's valuable possessions—small ones that were easy to transport and sell—were gone. When you came across a bill of sale from an antique shop for some of the missing items, your worst fears were confirmed. Sherry was stealing from your mother. Since then you haven't dared to confront her.

Clarify the Problem

1. Does everyone agree a problem exists?

You know your sister has been stealing from your mother, but you have not spoken with anyone about it. The problem is known only to you, therefore, and you must be the one to broach it.

2. How urgent is the problem, really?

The problem isn't urgent in the sense that your mother needs the missing items. However, it is a pressing problem because soon your mother will need the money the items could have provided to pay for her nursing home care.

3. What is behind your sister's problematic behavior?

As your mother's primary caregiver, Sherry may feel justified in taking and selling your mother's valuables. To her, these rewards could represent payback for all her work and devotion. In addition, although she hasn't said it, she may be angry that you have done far less for your mother than she has, and now she wants to make sure she is compensated.

4. What's hooking you?

Your reluctance to confront your sister is understandable. Having to accuse her of being a thief is an uncomfortable position to be in. Furthermore, you will have to reveal that you distrusted her enough to go behind her back. However, no matter how annoyed Sherry becomes, or how hard she tries to justify her actions, thievery is just that—a dishonorable act and a slap in the face to both you and your mother. In addition, there are practical implications. Your mother is not a wealthy woman. Sherry's thefts are a blow to your mother's financial well-being. You also are affected, since any shortfall in money needed for your mother's care will come partially out of your pocket.

5. Who must be included in problem-solving discussions?

You need to confront your sister and discuss what has been happening. Since your mother is bedridden and unaware of the thefts, there is no point in involving her. Although we generally advocate including your parents in any discussion that affects them, we are making an exception in this case. No real purpose will be served and a great deal of harm can be done by drawing her in.

6. What is your goal?

Your goal is to bring your sister's stealing to an end and have her make restitution to your mother.

Solve the Problem

1. Decide on the needs your solution must satisfy.

Your solution must enable your sister to pay back your mother, with either the cash equivalent of the missing valuables or the valuables themselves. Your solution must also allow Sherry to save face as well as provide a way for her to manage her anger and resentment in more constructive ways than stealing. Finally, your solution must spare all of you needless embarrassment.

2. Come up with a few possible solutions.

One solution is to talk candidly with your sister, confront her about the thefts, and work out a plan for restitution.

A second solution incorporates everything in the above solution but adds the urgent recommendation that she seek professional help before the situation gets worse.

A third solution—if a personal confrontation is not possible or is ineffective, and if seeking professional help is unacceptable to your sister—is to threaten to file a report with your state's Office of the Aging. (See *Elder Abuse, Neglect, and Exploitation* on page 205.)

3. Analyze the choices and select the best solution.

(See chart on next page.)

The best solution is to talk candidly with your sister. Whether you urge her to seek professional help depends on her response.

4. Conduct a Murphy's Law analysis.

If your sister won't discuss the matter with you or will not acknowledge her wrongdoing even in the face of the evidence you have accumulated, your preferred solution cannot work. If she continues to take your mother's things, you need to put her on notice that you will report her to state authorities. Such a threat may be sufficient to bring about a change of heart or at least a change of behavior.

GOAL: How can I get my sister to stop stealing and to make restitution to our mother?

	POSSIBLE SOLUTIONS			
NEEDS	Do nothing	Talk candidly with your sister	Talk candidly with your sister, and urge her to seek professional help	Threaten to file a report with your state's Office of the Aging
Must enable your sister to pay back your mother	no	yes, if you both agree on a plan	yes, if she agrees to a restitution plan	yes, but at the cost of your relationship with your sister once you follow through
Must allow your sister to save face	yes	yes, if the approach is sensitive to your sister's feelings	yes, if the approach is sensitive to your sister's feelings	no
Must allow your sister to express her anger and resentment in ways other than stealing	no	yes, if she is able to talk about her feelings	yes	eventually, if your sister is given the help she needs
Must spare the family needless embarrassment	yes	yes	probably	no

5. Carry out your plan.

Your task is complicated, since you have to confront Sherry without making her feel like a common thief. The best way to do this is to focus on your own hurt and dismay, and on your desire to understand her reasons and feelings. You might say something like, "Sherry, I hate even to have to say this, but I know you've been taking Mom's things. This isn't like you. What's going on?" Given the chance to talk, without fear of blame, she may tell you how burdened she has felt, and how angry she has been with you for leaving her with this responsibility. Expect her to feel upset at having been found out, even if she has justified her actions to herself.

Elder Abuse, Neglect, and Exploitation

Each state's Office of the Aging is charged with the responsibility of investigating any situation in which a senior is being victimized. There are three types of victimization:

- abuse—physical or psychological;

- neglect—by anyone, including themselves;

- exploitation—whether the senior is being stolen from, taken advantage of financially, made to provide services (such as child care) against his or her will, or used in other ways.

To file a complaint, call your state's Office of the Aging. This information can be found in your telephone directory or through your local senior center. You can also contact the National Association of Area Agencies on Aging at (202) 872-0888 or www.n4a.org/ and ask for the nearest Area Agency. An advisor at the Agency can put you in touch with the appropriate state authorities.

Your call will initiate an investigation. If the caseworker is able to verify your claim, steps will be taken immediately to bring the abuse, neglect, or exploitation to an end. Sometimes verification is not easy because seniors may be incapable of cooperating due to physical or mental limitations. Often they are unwilling to admit what has been happening, out of fear of reprisal or simply out of shame. In these cases, the investigations may take longer, and you may need to play a more active role in the interim.

Wrongdoers are usually treated with compassion. Unless they are professional exploiters, they are almost always given help rather than prosecuted. Nevertheless, the mere fact that they have been called to account makes the situation extremely agonizing for all involved.

Once the thefts are out in the open, you need to talk about restitution. Tell Sherry your concern about meeting your mother's future nursing home expenses, and work out a way for her to return the missing objects or give back the money obtained from their sale. Mention your desire to keep your mother ignorant of the thefts, so that no bridges are burned.

To prevent similar problems from arising in the future, you may need to take a more active role in your mother's care. Talk with your sister more regularly about how things are going so that her resentments do not build again. In addition, it may be time to start making more definite plans for your mother's nursing home admission.

6. Evaluate your progress.

In the short term, the matter will be settled once you and Sherry clear the air and restitution is made. You will know you have succeeded in the long term when you are convinced that Sherry is no longer taking your mother's things and when you and Sherry are able to reestablish a trusting relationship.

॒ॐ

My mother's handyman borrows money from her and doesn't pay her back.

Situation

Your 89-year-old mother lives alone in a small house about 45 minutes away from you. Although frail, she is strongly opposed to being "put away in a nursing home." She depends on her neighbor, Fred, to help her around the house. This pleasant, retired man mows her lawn in the summer, shovels her walk in the winter, and performs a variety of handyman tasks, from fixing leaky faucets to changing light bulbs. Fred is also good company for your mother. He often passes the time of day with her over a cup of coffee after he completes a job. She is grateful for all he does. She pays him well for his work, and both of them seem satisfied.

However, there is one problem. Fred is not well-off, and he frequently borrows small amounts of money from your mother—$10 here, $20 there. She tells you about these loans and seems a bit annoyed by the fact that Fred does not pay her back. However, she has never told him that he must do so. To date, he owes her almost two hundred dollars.

In the past, when you have pressed your mother to remind Fred about the money he owes her, she has become upset with you. She would rather let him have the money than make a scene and perhaps lose his help, without which she believes she would not be able to stay in her home.

Clarify the Problem

1. *Does everyone agree a problem exists?*

You and your mother agree there is a problem, but you disagree on what should be done about it, if anything.

2. *How urgent is the problem, really?*

The situation is not urgent, but it is irritating. Your mother is to some degree held hostage by her handyman and by her own thinking, since she believes she cannot stay in her home without his help. Furthermore, these small loans certainly will add up over time. The situation should not be allowed to continue.

3. *What is behind your mother's problematic behavior?*

Your mother needs Fred and wants to keep him happy so he will be available to help her. If lending him small amounts of money is a way to do that, it is no surprise that she is willing to do so. However, she never intended the loans to be outright gifts, and she is aware that he is taking advantage of her, either deliberately or unintentionally. Her fear is that if she confronts him and there is a scene, he will leave.

4. *What's hooking you?*

You feel angry that Fred is taking advantage of your mother, either intentionally or otherwise. Your annoyance at his not returning the borrowed money is compounded by the fact that you feel your hands are tied. You cannot *make* your mother confront him (she has said she does not want to). And to speak with him on your mother's behalf without her consent—an understandable urge—would be disrespectful to her and would undermine your relationship.

5. *Who must be included in problem-solving discussions?*

You and your mother are the only people who must agree on what to do about this problem.

6. What is your goal?

You would like to get Fred to pay back the money he borrowed. You would also like to bring an end to his borrowing.

Solve the Problem

1. Decide on the needs your solution must satisfy.

Your solution must keep the peace between your mother and Fred and not jeopardize her relationship with him. (If you get him to return the money, but he quits as her handyman, you cannot consider your solution successful.) It must also satisfy you that you have done all you reasonably can to remedy the situation and to protect your mother's interests.

2. Come up with a few possible solutions.

One option is to get your mother's permission to speak with Fred in order to find out why he has not returned the money he borrowed and to ask him to do so. Another option is to help your mother find an inoffensive excuse she can use to justify not lending him any more money. For example, she can tell him that you have forbidden her to lend money to anyone or that she has no cash on hand to lend. This doesn't resolve the issue of the money already lent, but it prevents the continuation of the problem.

3. Analyze your choices and select the best solution.

(See chart on next page.)

Both of your proposed strategies are necessary to resolve your dilemma completely.

4. Conduct a Murphy's Law analysis.

Because your mother relies on Fred, she may not give you permission to speak with him. If that happens, you have to forego trying to arrange for the return of her money. It is not a huge sum, and your mother's peace of mind is worth it.

GOAL: How can I get my mother's handyman to pay back the money he borrowed, and help my mother find a way to stop lending him more money?

	POSSIBLE SOLUTIONS		
NEEDS	Do nothing	With your mother's permission, find out why Fred has not returned the money he borrowed, and arrange for him to begin paying her back	Help your mother find an inoffensive excuse to justify not lending Fred more money
Must not jeopardize the relationship between your mother and Fred	no	yes, if you are tactful	probably
Must satisfy your need to know you have done all you can to protect your mother's interests	no	yes	yes

But you should still encourage her to stop lending Fred money at all.

This can lead to another problem. Suppose you and your mother decide that she will refuse Fred's requests for additional loans by offering a polite excuse that you and she come up with. What if she is not able to stand up to him when the time comes? If *that* occurs, you can offer to speak with Fred directly to ask that he stop borrowing money from your mother. You and your mother can agree on the reasons you give him.

If your mother is afraid that saying anything at all about the situation will antagonize Fred, you can help her see that it is Fred's *help*, not Fred himself, that she relies on. It may put her mind at ease if you offer to contact or give her the names and telephone numbers of individuals and agencies that provide the same kind of help as Fred does. (Low-cost "chore services" are available through many senior centers.) Knowing she has an alternative may make it possible for her to risk speaking with Fred.

5. Carry out your plan.

Since your mother agrees there is a problem, your main tasks are (1) to involve her in coming up with solutions that she will be willing to carry out, and (2) to motivate her to take action. You might accomplish both by saying something like this: "Mom, I know you like Fred and depend on what he does for you. But I also know you're annoyed that he never pays back any of the money he borrows. Let's see whether we can find a way to get the money back and put an end to his borrowing from you." By drawing her into the problem-solving process, you make it more likely that she will be willing to look at options.

You may want to offer to speak with Fred. Your doing so removes your mother from the awkward position of loan collector. It also makes it less likely that her relationship with Fred will be undermined. To sell this idea, you might say something like this: "Mom, I know the situation is awkward, and I'm sure you don't relish speaking with Fred yourself. Of course, you could do it. I know that. But how would you feel about my doing it for you? That way, if Fred gets upset, he will be upset with *me* and not you. You and I can agree in advance on what I will say. And when it's all over, he probably won't have bad feelings toward you."

6. Evaluate your progress.

You will have succeeded when Fred pays back the money he has borrowed and your mother stops lending him more.

There is an important additional consideration. Although Fred seems to be honest, he may be more of an exploiter than he appears. If that is the case, even if he stops borrowing money, he may try to take advantage of your mother in other ways. For example, he may borrow garden tools and neglect to return them, or convince her to give him small valuables, such as silver candlesticks she no longer uses. You and your mother must be on the lookout for signs of further exploitation and be prepared to act. If such behavior does occur, it is clear that the only real option is to fire Fred and find another solution.

DILEMMA TWENTY-FIVE

ᘰ

My father's frequent phone calls
are just too much.

Situation

You are married with three children, ages 8, 12, and 16. Your father, a healthy 72-year-old, lives alone several miles away. Widowed three years ago, he has done remarkably well since your mother's death. He is active in his senior center, and he is the president of the local chapter of AARP. He even has a woman friend, although you've never met her. You and various members of your family make sure to visit him every couple of weeks. He delights in seeing your children, and he gets along very well with you and your spouse.

Over the past month, for reasons you can't understand, he has begun calling several times a day. He speaks at length to whoever answers the phone and tries to keep that person on the line with him by asking innumerable questions and insisting on detailed answers. None of his calls are for anything urgent.

Your spouse is becoming impatient, and your children are complaining that they need the telephone to speak with their friends. You have told him he is calling too often and asked him to stop, but he keeps doing it anyway.

Clarify the Problem

1. Does everyone agree a problem exists?

Your family and you certainly feel that your father's calls are too frequent and too long. Your father, however, sees nothing wrong with wanting to "keep in touch."

2. How urgent is the problem, really?

There appears to be no immediate cause for alarm. Your father doesn't seem to be depressed. Aside from his frequent calling, he is behaving appropriately. (You would be more concerned, for example, if he were crying when he called or talking about life not being worth living.) Nonetheless, this change in his behavior troubles you, and you have a feeling that something is going on that he is not talking about.

3. What is behind your father's problematic behavior?

There has to be some cause for the change in your father's behavior. Lacking any real information, you can only make educated guesses. Perhaps he is lonely because his relationship with his lady friend has ended. Or perhaps he is experiencing a physical symptom that is frightening. Given the vast number of possibilities, you need more information to know with any certainty.

4. What's hooking you?

Because it is *your* father's behavior that is posing a problem for your family, you may feel responsible for making things right as quickly as possible. However, if you simply get him to stop calling, you may never discover what the real problem is.

You may also be reluctant to see your father as needing your help. You were probably relieved at his exceptional adjustment after your mother's death, and his self-sufficiency set up the expectation that you would not need to take care of him.

If your father has always been the one *you* go to with a problem, it may be difficult to see him as vulnerable and needing your help now.

5. Who must be included in problem-solving discussions?

You and your father are the only ones who should be involved in these discussions. Although your family is affected, if the cause of your father's behavior is a personal matter, he may be uncomfortable discussing it in front of everyone. If proposed solutions require your family's cooperation, they can be brought in at that time.

6. What is your goal?

You want to reduce the frequency and length of your father's calls, but you want to do so by addressing the underlying cause.

Solve the Problem

1. Decide on the needs your solution must satisfy.

Your solution must allow your family a reprieve from your father's too frequent calls. You must also find a way to uncover what is bothering him. Finally, whatever you decide to do, you must not risk hurting your father or making him feel that your family is unwilling to talk with him.

2. Come up with a few possible solutions.

One option is to ask your father to call at a specific time each day and to let him know that he is free to leave a message at other times.

A second option is to invite him to visit more often. Increasing the time he spends with you and your family might lessen his need to call so often.

A third option is to speak with your father about his frequent calls and try to find out *why* he needs to be in touch so often.

3. Analyze the choices and select the best solution.

GOAL: How can I reduce the frequency of my father's phone calls?

NEEDS	POSSIBLE SOLUTIONS			
	Do nothing	Limit his calls by setting specific times for him to call and having him leave a message at other times	Invite him to visit more often	Speak with him to find out why he is calling so often
Must reduce the frequency of your father's calls	no	yes	possibly, if it meets his need for more contact	yes, if it uncovers the reason behind his calls
Must help you understand why he is calling so often	no	no	no	yes
Must protect his feelings	yes	no	yes	possibly

Speaking with your father to learn why he is calling is clearly the preferred solution.

4. Conduct a Murphy's Law analysis.

Your preferred solution will work only if your father himself is aware of why he is calling and is willing to talk about it. If he is not sure why or is unwilling to talk, your problem is more difficult to solve. For example, suppose your father offers vague explanations that fail to make sense, such as saying he just wants to make sure you and the family are okay. Or suppose he denies that his calls are motivated by *any* concern or problem he has. Or what if he becomes annoyed with your bringing up the topic at all?

If any of these occur, you know that something more is going on than even he realizes. If this is the case and you try to confront him further, you will probably end up having an argument. For that reason, you would be wise to drop the issue for the time being. At some later date, you may want to bring it up again. Over time, whatever is going on might become clearer. In the meantime, you can still set limits on his calling and look for ways to increase contact with him, such as inviting him to visit or calling him more often.

5. Carry out your plan.

Your plan relies on your father's willingness to open up. Therefore, using communication strategies that will help him do this is crucial. Use *I*-messages such as these: "Dad, I'm concerned that you've been calling more often than you usually do. I'm wondering if there's something going on that we should talk about." Messages like this let your father know how you are feeling, without blaming him. They also invite him to disclose information that can help you understand the reason behind his calls. (See pages 12–13 for more information on *I*-messages.)

Your father may respond in a number of ways. For example, he might say, "I didn't realize until lately how much I miss your mother." Or he might tell you about a health concern or the end of a romance. It may be that despite his active lifestyle, he has few people to talk to about intimate concerns. Or perhaps he has tried talking with friends and has been given platitudes, such as, "Don't worry, you'll get over it." Your simple act of listening may be all that is needed. However, if he needs help dealing with a matter of concern to him, you can offer him specific advice or find someone who can assist him.

This conversation should occur in person, not over the telephone, so that you can pay attention to his appearance and behavior while you are talking with him. If he looks uncomfortable or distressed, this can confirm your suspicion that *something* is bothering him. For example, suppose you ask whether he is lonely. He flinches for a moment, then quickly says, "No, no! I have lots to keep me busy." This response, just a bit too emphatic to be convincing, leaves you feeling that he is covering up.

While you may not be able to say anything more at the moment, you may be able to find ways to help him with his problem, without his having to confront it. For example, if you suspect that he is lonely, you can invite him to have dinner with your family more often. If, however, the problem seems to be more complex—such as depression or a serious health problem—then you will need to get him to acknowledge the problem and convince him to get help.

6. Evaluate your progress.

You will know you have succeeded when your father returns to a more normal pattern of calling, shows no signs of distress, and continues to have a close relationship with your family.

The Caring Partnership

❧

CHAPTER SIX

Avoiding Blunders

Preventing Problems Before They Arise

Up to this point, everything you're read in this book has focused on helping you manage conflicts that develop between you and your aging parents. But what if you could avoid these conflicts in the first place? What if you could establish a mutually respectful relationship in which both you and your parents take responsibility for dealing with the various dilemmas that inevitably arise as parents age? We call such a relationship a *caring partnership*.

We know that most children and parents are well-intentioned. Nevertheless, both parties often wind up feeling hurt and distressed.

- Conscientious children, acting out of kindness, help parents and expect appreciation; they are startled when, instead, they encounter anger and resistance.

- Sensitive parents, determined to avoid burdening their children, take pride in their self-sufficiency. If they accept help they do not want, they feel resentful and diminished; if they refuse, they are seen as ungrateful and stubborn.

We added this chapter because of our conviction that if you understand what goes wrong between parents and children you can avoid needless conflicts in the first place. To the extent that you can "partner" with your parents in making decisions about their care, you'll be able to offer better, more timely help, with less conflict and aggravation. This chapter will give you the tools you need to weather most conflicts successfully and to avoid needless ones altogether.

Three Basic Errors Well-Meaning Children Make

When introducing our Problem-Solving Model, we brought up the concept of urgency (pages 30–31). *Subjective* urgency is the feeling that something *must* be done right away to correct a situation the adult child finds distressing. For example, you may be upset by your healthy parent's refusal to eat a well-rounded diet. While this may be distressing, it is not an urgent matter. (By contrast, *objective* urgency is just what it sounds like: a feeling of pressure born of undeniable facts, as when a parent's failure to take medication as prescribed results in the development of a life-threatening condition.)

The feeling of subjective urgency is at the heart of the first two basic errors well-meaning children make: they act prematurely, and they fail to consider their parents' needs and desires. In both cases, because of their *own* distress, children forget to treat their parents courteously and respectfully.

1. Children act prematurely.

In the course of an interview that occurred not long after the original publication of *Are Your Parents Driving You Crazy?* a reporter told us she was very distressed over her 75-year-old father's driving between Florida and New York several times a year. "He's just too old to be driving such distances," she said. When we asked about his driving record, she admitted it was perfect. Nevertheless, she had urged him to confine his driving to local roads because she worried to death each time he drove. "It's a long trip," she said, "and I can't imagine he can drive it

222

safely." Understandably, her father had refused to listen to her. He saw no reason why he shouldn't do what he did well and enjoyed doing. Moreover, he was put off by his daughter's unwanted advice and offended at her judgment that he couldn't drive safely anymore.

Many children confuse objective and subjective urgency. If our reporter's father had had several accidents, or if he had received more than one summons for unsafe driving, his daughter's alarm would have been understandable. However, that was not the case. Her worry was tied solely to her father's age. The urgency she felt was entirely of her making.

Acting in haste can also lead children to take action before clarifying just what the problem really is. In their rush to find solutions, they provide the wrong kind of help. Susan, for example, a woman speaking with us after a presentation, panicked when her 85-year-old mother complained that her house was hot and stuffy. Having recently read that older people may have trouble coping with temperature extremes, she envisioned her mother lying on the floor, hot and dehydrated. "I rushed to the store," she told us, "bought the best air conditioner they had, and arranged for installation that very day." She called her mother to tell her what she did, and paid scant attention to her mother's response, "Thanks, but you really didn't have to do that." Two days later, on a hot, humid day, she called her mother to find out how things were going, expecting to be praised for her thoughtfulness. To her dismay, her mother was not using the air conditioner. Susan was furious. "You told me you were hot and uncomfortable," she fumed. "Now you won't use the air conditioner. What's going on?" Quietly, her mother explained that the house was hot and stuffy because the windows had swollen from humidity and she was unable to open them. All she had needed was someone to free up the windows so she could get some fresh air. In rushing to action, Susan had misunderstood her mother's problem and then came up with a solution that went far beyond her mother's actual needs.

2. Children fail to consider their parents' feelings and desires.

When well-meaning children see their parents struggling, whether the struggle involves doing a job around the house or managing some other aspect of their lives, most cannot just stand by. In their haste to help, they fail to ask whether their parents *want* help. They forget that their parents are people with feelings and needs of their own—people who have been running their own lives for a long time. For the parents, the struggle to do a job may be preferable to accepting help.

One woman, a nurse, told us about a tragic turn of events in her family. Her mother was dying of cancer. Although she needed round-the-clock care, she preferred to remain at home. Her three daughters, all licensed nurses, wanted to take care of her themselves. To them, providing care was more than an act of loving compassion; it was a way of sparing their mother the need to adjust to stranger-caregivers, and it would save money besides. Their mother refused their offer. She was, after all, their mother, she told them; she did not want them bathing and diapering her. Unable to understand her refusal, and out of a sincere desire to help, her daughters prevailed on her until their mother finally relented. However, she found their involvement humiliating, not comforting. She made it clear during the weeks before her death that they had done her a gross disservice. "We only wanted to do what we thought was best for her," the nurse told us. "But to this day we regret what we did. We'd have been far smarter to listen to her and respect her wishes. She paid for our help with her self-respect." Ironically, the woman's children would have done far more by doing less.

When children ignore a parent's feelings they increase the likelihood that their help will be unappreciated—or worse, rejected—even if it is needed. A man named Brian told us that he had experienced this first-hand. Several months earlier, his elderly mother reported that she had slipped and almost fallen the previous night as she was getting out of the bathtub. Brian knew about grab bars and the important part they play in helping to prevent falls. Alarmed, he lost no time contacting a carpenter. Within a week grab bars had been installed. "Now, Mom," he said proudly when the job was done, "you can get out of the tub safely." To his dismay, his mother pronounced the grab bars "institutional" and said she'd rather take sponge baths than have her house look like a nursing home. In his haste to take care of his mother, Brian had ignored her feelings and preferences. "If I could do it over again," he remarked, "I would have asked for her permission to install the bars. I'd even have had her choose the style she wanted."

Good intentions like Brian's are lost sight of when children override parents' wishes or try to impose their will. Regardless of how they pressure parents—whether through logical argument, coercion, threats, intimidation, or manipulation—the very act of imposing pressure offends parents. Angered, they understandably become resistant and oppositional. Children then become even more frustrated. Both sides prepare for battle. More often than not, the adversarial stance taken by each side sharply reduces any chance of arriving at a peaceful solution to the problem at hand. The stance can also poison the relationship permanently.

In our view, untold damage has been done by self-appointed experts in the field of eldercare, who glibly announce that as parents age children inevitably "become their parents' parents." We disagree. In our opinion, *children never become their parents' parents.* They may become their parents' helpers. They may offer advice, give them information about resources, and help them in other ways. They may even become hands-on caregivers. But they do not become their parents. Nor should they try to, *ever*.

Parents who are mentally intact have the absolute right to be included in any decisions that affect them. There's a maxim that captures this sentiment. It is: "Nothing about me without me." We feel strongly that to succeed as caregivers of aging parents, adult children must remember this principle. Chances are very good that whether your parents express this view explicitly or not, they believe in it: *Nothing about me without me.*

We recognize that in some cases parents simply cannot participate in decisions about their care. For example, they may be incapable of thinking rationally, perhaps as a result of dementia or another incapacitating illness. In such cases it only makes sense for children to take over. However, contrary to what many people believe, the vast majority of aging parents are *not* demented. That's why it is both proper and respectful for children to ask parents about their wishes, and to comply with them, even if the children disagree.

This is a worthwhile distinction to bear in mind. The mere fact that children and parents disagree doesn't in any way justify concluding that parents are incapable of sound thinking. People of all ages see things differently. Disagreement itself doesn't mean one side is "right" and the other "wrong." Especially if you are an adult child, we caution you to avoid equating differences of opinion with proof that your parents are incapable of being reasonable.

3. Children do more than is needed.

So far we've talked about errors made by children because of their feelings of subjective urgency. The next basic error is born of something closely related but not quite the same. Swept up by caring and a desire to do all they can for the parents, the children go beyond the specific problem their parents may have asked them to solve and take on more responsibility than they should.

Here's what we mean. Mrs. Olins, at 93, could not make sense out of the bill she had received from the heating oil company she did business with. The company had instituted a "budget plan," also known as a "level billing plan." The plan required a monthly payment whether or not heating oil was delivered. This made no sense to Mrs. Olins. Fearful that she was being overcharged, she asked her son to try to straighten things out. The son agreed that the bill was confusing. He called the heating oil company. The representative reviewed the way the billing system worked and confirmed that everything was in order. Mrs. Olins's son could have stopped right there and explained the "level billing" system to his mother. After all, he had done what she had asked. Instead, he decided to write out the check to the heating oil company. Then he went even further. "Mom," he suggested, "as long as I'm writing this check out, why don't I pay the rest of your bills? Maybe I can save you some work." His mother handed over her checkbook. The son, pleased to help, wrote several checks. The following month, he found to his dismay that his mother (perhaps to please her son) had not paid *any* bills on her own. Instead, she had gathered them up and left them for her son to pay. He discovered, too late, that by giving help beyond what had been asked for, he had solved one problem but created another. Without intending to, he had taken on a monthly burden and had simultaneously undermined his mother's self-sufficiency.

Four Basic Errors Parents Make

Despite what some frustrated children might think, parents don't set out to drive them crazy. The overwhelming majority of parents just want to be allowed to enjoy the independence they are accustomed to. When it comes to accepting help, parents appreciate their children's concern but resent help when it is intrusive. They may be grateful when help is offered but indignant when it is imposed. They welcome suggestions but only when asked for.

However, parents may also behave in ways that actually fuel conflicts with their children. There are four primary ways parents do this: by disregarding the consequences of the risks they take, by refusing to face facts, by withholding information, and by behaving provocatively.

1. *Parents fail to consider the consequences of risks they take.*

Ironically, parents sometimes make things worse precisely when they try hardest not to. This point was brought home to us by an incident involving our 80-year-old neighbor and her two children.

The curtains on our neighbor's kitchen window needed changing. A proud and independent woman, she tackled the job herself rather than ask her children for help. (Because our neighbor is a small woman, and because the window is located over the sink, doing the job involved stepping onto a chair, climbing onto the counter, and actually *standing in the sink* to reach the curtain rod!) When her children visited, she couldn't wait to show them her new curtains. Asked who had changed them, she proudly said she had. How? they asked. She told them, expecting to be praised. Rather than admiring her self-sufficiency, however, they became angry with her.

The woman was hurt and shocked. From her point of view, her children's anger wasn't warranted. After all, she had done the job safely. More important, her intentions were good: she was taking care of things without imposing on her children. This seemed to be a good thing. Why, then, were they furious?

From her children's perspective, the woman had shown extremely poor judgment by jeopardizing her safety for something as trivial as kitchen curtains. Their concern for her safety far outweighed any pleasure in her accomplishment. In fact, they had a point. As someone ages, many tasks become riskier. Standing on a chair and climbing onto a counter and into a sink might pose only a minimal danger for a 40-year-old: balance is better, and the consequences of a fall are less serious. However, balance is usually poorer at age 80, and broken bones take longer to heal.

The children were upset not just because they feared for their mother's welfare but also they feared for their own. After all, if she had been injured, *they* would have been affected too.

When older parents fail to consider the consequences of their actions, they are inviting conflict. When they put themselves at risk, they do more than frighten, distress, and anger the children; they cause them to lose faith in their parents' judgment. When children begin questioning their parents' every action, the stage is set for discord.

2. Parents refuse to face facts.

Some parents fuel conflicts by refusing to acknowledge problems, even though the evidence may be staring them in the face. Dilemma sixteen (pages 150–157), which details the case of a well-spouse who would not accept help despite his inability to care for his wife, is typical. In situations like that one, parents' refusal to face facts compounds the problems of eldercare. When offers of needed help are rejected, children become concerned, frustrated, and eventually angry. They begin seeing their parents as problems rather than as people. Conflict becomes almost inevitable.

Should this happen in your family, keep the following two facts in mind. First, the refusal to face facts is often borne of *fear*. Many elderly parents have told us they worry that if they acknowledge that they need help of any kind, they will lose control over their lives.

Second, the refusal to see the truth may also be the result of an automatic process called *denial*. Faced with a situation that is difficult or unpleasant to accept, parents may overlook hard facts, such as diminished vision, hearing, or balance, and insist that nothing has changed. Based on this erroneous evaluation, they insist on doing what they have always done—cleaning the gutters each spring and fall, for example—regardless of the potential risks for themselves and consequences for their children.

Being sensitive to what is behind your parents' apparent stubbornness or unreasonableness is the first step in breaking the impasse. By empathizing with their fear, and by recognizing that their denial is a coping mechanism, you can see their behavior in a new light. As a consequence, you can offer the reassurance they need. In your words and actions, you can make it clear that your goal is to help them, not to run their lives. By indicating that you know your place—that you are their ally, their *caring partner,* you increase the likelihood that your parents will take a more reasonable look at your concerns, and accept your help.

3. Parents withhold information.

Sometimes well-meaning parents try to protect their children by keeping secrets. The experience of a woman named Barbara makes the point. Barbara lived about an hour from her father, a 79-year-old widower. She usually visited on Saturdays, helping him shop, doing some cooking for him, and lending a hand in other ways. During one visit she and her father had lunch, took a walk in a local park, and then did some shopping. Barbara helped him unpack groceries, and she started dinner for him. Everything seemed fine, and by mid-afternoon, they said their goodbyes and Barbara drove home feeling happy and fulfilled. When she got home, however, she found a message on her answering machine. It was from a nurse affiliated with the hospital in her father's area. He had gone to the emergency room on his own less than thirty minutes after she left. His primary symptom was chest pain. According to the nurse, preliminary indications were that her father had suffered a mild heart attack. Frightened and upset, Barbara drove back to the hospital at once. "Dad," she said when she finally got to speak with him, "were you in pain when we were together?" He said he had been. "Then why didn't you tell me?" she asked. His answer was: "I didn't want to worry you."

Withholding information may seem sensible to parents who don't want to trouble their children. However, in many instances, especially where important matters such as health are involved, children feel *entitled* to know what's going on. When parents keep secrets, their credibility is lost. As a result, children are likely to take it upon themselves to determine whether a need exists and to take whatever action they feel is necessary. Parents see this behavior as intrusive, and become angry. An adversarial relationship develops. Each side justifies its position: children view their parents as untrustworthy; parents see *them* as disrespectful. Both sides feel hurt, misunderstood, unappreciated, and angry.

As a result, impasses develop and communication grinds to a halt. Children say, "My parents are driving me crazy." Parents say, "My children are driving me crazy." In a sense, both are right. Each misunderstanding adds an additional layer of complexity to an already difficult situation. The ability to work together constructively is lost.

4. Parents behave in provocative ways.

Sometimes parents behave in ways that are almost certain to aggravate their children. For example, conflicts often develop when parents refuse to spend even modest amounts of money on themselves. One man told us his mother's scrimping is all the more upsetting because it is completely unnecessary. "My mother is fairly well off," he said. "My father left her well provided for. But for some reason she's decided to save every nickel she can. At the supermarket she buys day-old baked goods and reduced-price vegetables in dented cans. She even buys cold-cut ends to save a few pennies!" The man was not just embarrassed by his mother's tightfistedness; he was angry about it. "I worry about her getting sick on spoiled food," he said.

We suspect that this woman would do anything to avoid becoming a financial drain on her children; her penny-pinching is her way of ensuring that she does not. What she doesn't realize is just how upsetting her behavior is to her son.

Parents also provoke in other ways. We know one son who lives several hundred miles from his mother and can visit only a few times a year. He's told us that every time he speaks with his mother on the phone, she bombards him with a long list of tasks that need to be done around her home. "The windows need a good cleaning," she tells him. "The lawn is overgrown. The front steps need repair. The roof looks bad." The son says that he used to offer to set aside time to do the jobs. She always refused. "Hearing her complain and then turn down my offers of help was so infuriating I've stopped listening to her complaints."

Not knowing his mother, we can't gauge her motivations. It's possible she simply needs someone to listen to her and empathize. Or, she may be angry with her son because he visits infrequently. Whatever her reasons, there's no doubt that her provocative behavior contributes to bad feelings between the two of them and makes meaningful collaboration impossible.

What to Do:
The Problem-Avoiding Model

Regardless of where problems begin or who is to blame, the effect is the same: conflicts develop that drive wedges between children and parents. Both sides read arrogance into efforts to be helpful. They hear insults where none are intended. Children mistake determination for willfulness. Parents mistake caring for intrusiveness. Children feel deceived by parents' efforts to spare them worry. Parents sense condescension when children mean only to be kind. What can be done? We believe the answer lies in revisiting the first part of our Problem-Solving Model—clarifying the problem—and applying it in a slightly different way. We recommend that you use the "clarify the problem" section of our model to prevent problems from occurring in the first place. Think of this as our Problem-Avoiding Model.

1. Is any action really needed?

Before saying anything to your parents about a problem you think exists, ask yourself the following questions.

Have there been any verifiable facts or events that have caused me concern? By examining the situation carefully in order to be certain a real problem exists, you do yourself two favors. First, scrutiny helps you to be certain you are operating on the basis of objective, not subjective, urgency. Second, having facts in hand puts you in a much sounder position to convince your parents that a problem exists, if, indeed, you must convince them of that.

For example, suppose you are concerned about how your parents are managing their own finances. You know they are forgetful and you worry about the possibility that they may mislay letters and bills. Arguing in the abstract about their ability to manage money could be fruitless. However, if creditors have begun calling or if your parents have begun receiving threatening letters from collection agencies, you have objectively verifiable evidence that something needs to be done.

Are there any changes I've noticed that my parents may not be aware of? Because problems sometimes develop slowly, people very close to a situation may fail to see lapses that are readily apparent to others. Deterioration in personal habits or physical surroundings, for example, tends to occur in such small increments that parents may be completely unaware of it. If you have not seen your parents for a while, you may be stunned at what you observe. This is one reason why holidays may be difficult. Relatives who visit only periodically may be struck by the changes that have occurred since the last visit. Coming on like gangbusters, however, and demanding that changes occur immediately will only create bad feelings and resistance. It is hard for anyone, when distressed, to remain composed and to plan an effective strategy. To regain perspective, keep in mind that very few situations are life-threatening. If problematic changes have occurred, you must be able to describe them without becoming angry or emotional, and you need to rely on facts that your parents cannot overlook. By sharing your concern in a noncritical manner, you may be able to convince your parents to work with you to solve the problem.

Do I have important information my parents lack? Chances are, if you are reading this book, you try to stay informed about matters pertaining to the care of aging parents. In the course of doing that, you may uncover information that has implications for your parents and indicates a need for action.

For example, in the course of reading an article in a local newspaper you may realize that your parents' living wills are out of date. Perhaps you've learned that your state has instituted new requirements or that a more detailed form is available. The "problem" in this case has less to do with how your parents are functioning than with legal matters that can create problems down the road. It is appropriate for you to make your parents aware that their advance directives must be brought up to date.

If your parents are like most people, they will not be thrilled when you bring up the topic. Talking about advance directives is inherently distasteful because the topic raises issues of death and dying. While there is no easy solution, the best way to approach this topic is by explaining your concern, and indicating your awareness of the unpleasantness of dealing with such matters. Remind your parents that these documents help them to stay in control of their lives for as long as they are alive. It would also be a good idea to have the new forms on hand, and even better if you have executed them for yourself first.

In the previous examples, we've assumed that the problems you identified were clear. We now turn to situations that are less transparent. We're thinking of situations in which you cannot clearly identify a reason for intervening; nevertheless, you feel a distinct sense that something needs to be done.

2. Do I feel a need to do something, but lack compelling objective evidence that a problem exists?

If you feel the need to do something, but cannot explain why, look carefully at what may really be going on. Understanding your motives can help you avoid blunders such as acting prematurely, without understanding your parents' needs.

Almost always the feeling that you must do something originates from one of three sources. First, it may stem from your own needs. When this occurs, any action that is taken is not likely to be necessary, or even in the parents' best interest. For example, if you believe that caring children should have their aging parents live with them, you may be tempted to pressure your parents into selling their home and moving in with you. Below we will help you gauge the extent to which the desire to intervene is borne of your own needs.

Second, your feeling may stem from external factors that are affecting your thinking and judgment. For example, you may have had a conversation with a friend whose parents have just moved to an assisted living facility and who is convinced that everyone's parents should follow suit, making you feel that you'd better discuss this with your own parents as soon as possible. Or, an article you've read about supplements to prevent memory loss may cause you to feel neglectful if you don't bring this to your parents' attention. If this is what is underlying your feelings of urgency, there's a step (that we'll give you further below) that can prevent your taking action without thinking, or involving your parents in unnecessary discussions and decisions.

Third, you may feel that some action on your part is called for because your parents have indicated indirectly that they need help. For example, your mother may have complained about how dim the living room lights seem. Your father may complain about how badly lit the local roads are. In this case, a sense that some action is needed is right on the mark. We'll give you an easy way to determine this.

MOTIVATING SOURCE ONE:
URGENCY ORIGINATING FROM INTERNAL SOURCES
To determine whether your desire to do something stems from your own needs, ask yourself the following two questions: *What will happen if I do nothing?* and *How will I feel if I do nothing?* This pair of questions is the simplest and best way we know to gauge

whether you are operating on the basis of subjective urgency. If you find that nothing terrible will occur if you do nothing, but you still feel the need to do something, stop right there! Instead of acting, or offering advice, or lecturing your parents, try to figure out where the pressure is coming from. You may be caught in an emotional "hook" having nothing directly to do with your parents' current situation. Pages 33 and 35 gave some examples of hooks. In the following paragraphs we expand on this concept.

You may be motivated by the fear that others will think of you as uncaring. It's a fact that some people do stand in judgment of adult children. You know best whether in your life there is a critical relative, family friend, or even a neighbor whose opinion matters disproportionately to you. Despite the fact that you know they lack the details of your parents' needs, you may nevertheless imagine them judging you harshly unless you do what you feel they think you "should." The fear of their criticism may push you toward premature action, or even action against your better judgment.

You may be in competition with your siblings or others, seeking to prove yourself the good child, or the best, the most caring, or the most devoted. Rivalries with siblings rarely disappear completely, even in adulthood; we've observed that they are often intensified under the stress of eldercare-giving. You may even imagine finally winning out over rivals for your parents' affection. Decisions motivated by needs stemming from long-standing rivalries are not likely to be sound ones. Even if they are, the friction that results is never in a parent's best interest.

You may be trying to atone for distress you caused your parents in the past. Attainment of adulthood gives children a new perspective on earlier behaviors. Actions that seemed justifiable at the time, like leaving home abruptly, dropping out of school, or getting involved in bad relationships, may cause feelings of shame and regret. Often, as parents age, and children see these once-invincible figures becoming old and frail, they desire to atone for past wrongs, to be forgiven and have the slate wiped clean. While improved and caring relationships are certainly a worthy goal, they cannot be achieved by imposing unwanted or unneeded help. In this case, it is important to acknowledge the need, but equally important to find a more realistic way to satisfy it.

You may be trying to elicit from your parents feelings of love and regard you never experienced. Perhaps your parents never felt warmly toward you for reasons of their own. Or even if they did, perhaps they were unable to express those feelings. Some children spend years trying to get what is assumed to be a childhood entitlement. Unfortunately, people tend not to change in basic ways. If your parents have always tended to be critical or reserved, there may be little or nothing you can do at this point. Nonetheless, you may imagine that if you do enough, work hard enough, give them enough, you will *finally* get it right. If this is your situation, you may need to face the sad truth that you may never get what you want from your parents, although you may be able to get it from a loving partner or friend.

As the previous four possibilities indicate, there are many motivations that fuel feelings of subjective urgency. Yours may be completely different from those of others. Our discussion is intended only to suggest some of the more common ones. Only careful self-examination will make it possible for you to uncover yours.

MOTIVATING SOURCE TWO:
URGENCY ORIGINATING FROM EXTERNAL SOURCES
To gauge whether your desire to do something for your parents has been triggered by some experience not directly connected with them, ask this question: *Have I been exposed to any influences lately that may have left me feeling I should do something?* As we

mentioned above, sometimes reading or hearing about eldercare options leaves you feeling that you should be doing something. Even hearing about what someone else is doing for their parents can make you feel you are being remiss. For example, a friend might tell you that at her prodding her parents finally agreed to accept in-home help. As a result their lives have improved a great deal. You feel remiss that you have not done what she has done and start wondering things like, "What's wrong with me? Why haven't I arranged for this?" In fact, the difficulties your friend's parents were facing may not be comparable to your parents' situation at all. Your friend's intervention may not even have been the best move to make. Regardless of any apparent parallels between situations, it would be difficult to know for sure whether in-home help would be appropriate for your parents.

In cases like this, acting impulsively, out of guilt, based on what someone *else* has done for *their* parents, is almost certainly a mistake. Instead, if you think there is merit in what your friend has done, talk with your parents. Tell them about what your friend has arranged and how you'd like to do as much for them as your friend is doing for his or her parents. See how your parents react, and what they think of the idea. If it seems appropriate, you might even ask about other forms of help as well. This strategy encourages your parents to let you know if there's anything they would like you to do for them that might make their lives easier or more pleasant. By proceeding in this manner, you can relieve yourself of a sense of guilt and urgency without imposing on your parents something that may not be wanted or needed.

MOTIVATING SOURCE THREE:
URGENCY ORIGINATING FROM AN INDIRECT MESSAGE FROM
YOUR PARENTS

To confirm whether your desire to do something for your parents has been triggered by an indirect communication from them, ask this question: *Have my parents indicated indirectly, through tone of voice, body language, or in some other way (for example, reporting to me about an incident involving someone else) that they need something from me but are unable to ask?* Like most of us, parents are often reluctant to ask for help directly. Their fear of imposing on children may inhibit any direct requests. However, if they really need something they may resort to hinting at it.

For example, one man told us his mother complained that she was having trouble reaching canned goods and other grocery items where they were stored in her kitchen, in cabinets above the counters. She could no longer easily climb and reach for them. Since she was not the kind of woman to make idle chatter or to complain, he sensed she was asking for something. He asked whether she would like him to look into some other ways of storing groceries, and she said she would. After a little research, he identified several storage options. He gathered literature from a local store and showed them to his mother. They agreed on a functional metal shelving unit that could be installed at a comfortable height on the back of a door that led to an attic stairway. In a matter of a few days, the man bought and installed the shelving unit and transferred the inaccessible grocery items to it. The problem was solved. His mother was grateful, and he was pleased with himself. This was all possible because he had listened to his mother's words and asked the right questions to meet the need with the appropriate action.

3. How are my parents likely to respond to my suggestions?

Even under the best of circumstances, and regardless of the reasons behind your desire to intervene on your parents' behalf, it is absolutely critical to anticipate your parents' reactions to your words and actions. If you're at all attuned to them you know their sore spots and vulnerabilities. For example, if your dad is an independent spirit, proud of his ability to drive, then issues having to do with the car will be problematic. If your mom always took pride in keeping a spotless home, then suggesting cleaning help is not likely to be welcome. Your knowledge of your parents, paired with what you've learned about the realities of aging, should give you some indication of how welcome particular suggestions are likely to be. When you understand where a reaction is coming from, you're less likely to feel hurt or distressed when your well-meaning help is rejected. Ask yourself the following questions.

How do my parents typically respond to any suggestions? Many parents deeply resent having their judgment questioned. Whether the issue is diet, spending patterns, transportation options, exercise (or lack thereof), or anything else, the mere fact that you question their judgment is reason enough for an argument. Knowing this, plan your persuasive approach carefully. Anticipate reactions, prepare your rejoinders, and do your best to keep the discussion on an even keel. You may not succeed, but the results are likely to be better than if you were to push ahead carelessly, just hoping for the best.

Is the topic I am going to bring up a known sore spot for them? Perhaps money is a hot topic for your parents and anything having to do with it is likely to trigger strong emotional reactions. Before venturing into areas that will most certainly create conflict, be sure that the payoff will be worth the effort. If you decide to go ahead, be sure to prepare yourself for the expected reactions, and be sure that you have a sound, fact-based line of argument to offer.

Is the topic I am going to bring up inherently upsetting? Some topics, such as death and dying, are difficult for anyone to discuss. People vary in how they show their distress. Some, for example, get visibly upset and cry. Your parents may even turn on you in a critical manner just to shut you up. Or they may make light of your earnest efforts in an attempt to avoid the subject. If you anticipate such reactions, then take proactive measures. For instance, introduce the subject with *I messages* (see pages 12–13). By doing so, you stand a better chance of getting a discussion started.

The Caring Partnership

Terms such as *eldercare* and *caregiving* both imply that only one person, the "giver" (or "carer" as they say in England) is active. In this traditional model, someone gives care, and someone receives it.

We believe that successful eldercare, especially when parents are competent, is not a one-way street. Rather, it is the result of a cooperative relationship between parent and child, where ideas and concerns are shared, and mutually satisfactory solutions are achieved. Reality, of course, usually falls short of this ideal. However, we believe that by following our suggestions and strategies, any adult child and older parent can improve the working relationship between them immeasurably. In the chapters that follow, we show how our approach can be applied to a variety of situations. Our emphasis here is on nurturing a caring partnership while resolving eldercare dilemmas.

CHAPTER SEVEN

Working with Your Parents

More Dilemmas and Solutions

In this chapter, we have compiled questions and comments frequently voiced since *Are Your Parents Driving You Crazy?* was first published. Some of them came from readers, others from members of audiences we've addressed, still others from radio and TV interviewers and their listeners and viewers. Where possible, we have used them to show you how to promote a caring partnership.

1. You've written the wrong book! You should have written, "Are Your Children Driving You Crazy?"

This comment was uttered by an elderly woman who called in during an interview on a talk radio station. She explained that she had been widowed a year or so earlier, but she had many friends in the community and was perfectly capable of running her life and managing her home. However, her children were hounding her to sell the house and either come live with one of them or move to an assisted living facility. The woman wanted no part of their plans. But no matter how often she told them she wanted to stay right where she was, and reassured them that she was doing fine, they would not listen.

Our Understanding: Her children's urgings were clearly a

product of their uneasiness. If the caller were to acquiesce and leave her home, she would be doing it to satisfy *their* needs rather than hers. If you find yourself running into conflict because you are urging something on your parents that they don't want, take a step back and ask yourself, "Whose needs are primary here?" Remember, your job is to help, not to take over.

2. It's my __father__ who's impossible. Why are you telling __me__ to get help?

Following a talk we gave at a senior center, a gentleman raised his hand and told of the futility of trying to take care of his rude and uncooperative father. Since he was clearly at the end of his rope, we suggested that the support of a professional helper might give him an opportunity to manage his frustration before it turned to anger. To our surprise, the man was enraged and offended by our recommendation.

Our Understanding: Many people, unfortunately, regard seeking professional help as a sign of failure or weakness. We were not suggesting that this man was "crazy" or that the problem was his fault. On the contrary, our recommendation was based on the realization that sometimes there is nothing an adult child can do to make a parent "come around." To expect gratitude from a person who is incapable of it is like waiting for an apple tree to grow oranges. In such cases, adult children bear the additional burdens of frustration, lack of gratification, and a sense of personal failure. When there is likely to be little or no relief forthcoming, seeking help for one's self is often the sensible thing to do.

3. [This] book is disrespectful to parents because it lays the blame for problems squarely on us.

These words appeared in a letter to the editor a few days after the *New York Times* published a positive review of our book. Basing her reaction solely on the title, the woman who wrote the letter faulted the book as reflecting the disdain with which some younger people view elderly parents.

Our Understanding: This woman had jumped to the conclusion that our book was "anti-parent." Nothing could be further from the truth. As we hope you've realized by now, one of the key themes of this book is respect. Without respect a child cannot establish a good working relationship with his or her parents. Regardless of their age or level of infirmity, your parents remain your parents. They should always be shown the respect they deserve. Anything less is not only insulting, it invites disaster.

Of course, when health and safety are seriously at risk, or when a parent's ability to reason is compromised by dementia or psychological factors, it may be necessary to exert pressure, even (in extreme cases) to countermand a parent's wishes. But such heavy-handed approaches are always regrettable and should be reserved for true emergencies. (And remember, this book is written with cognitively intact parents in mind.)

4. *When my mother was diagnosed with dementia, my wife and I built a new wing on our house so she could live with us. Now it turns out that her dementia is worse than we thought. She wanders into our bedroom every night and disrupts our family life in other ways. We're afraid to leave her alone during the day. What should we do?*

This dilemma was presented during a post-presentation Q&A, by a well-meaning and caring son who had overestimated his mother's ability to function.

Our Understanding: All too often, eldercare decisions are made without carefully considering the consequences. Had this man and his wife taken the time to learn about dementia, they would have realized that by the time the wing was built, it might be too late. In general, before offering to have a parent live with you, it is crucial to consider whether that arrangement will really solve the problem. In this case, we would recommend that the couple hire a well-trained aide to oversee the mother's care. If appropriate help isn't available, or if it proves inadequate, a move to an assisted living facility with a dementia unit would seem appropriate.

5. *My father can no longer drive, and occasionally asks us to buy him trivial items, such as lightbulbs and paper towels, while we're shopping. We are financially comfortable and can easily afford to pay for what we get him. But he insists on paying us back for every little thing. I don't want to take his money, but when I refuse, we end up in an argument.*

This conscientious son, aware of his father's limited financial resources, was frustrated by his efforts to make his father's life easier. He felt guilty taking the money but hated the battles that ensued if he refused.

Our Understanding: Our questioner missed the fact that his father's pride was at stake. It was painful enough for his father not to be able to drive to the store to buy the items himself, but worse when he was not permitted to pay for them. Given the many possible areas of conflict that arise as parents age, this is a good one to remove from the list. To help the son cope with his guilt at taking his father's money, we suggested that he set it aside in a special account for his father, to be "returned" in the form of thoughtful gifts or in other ways that would not be provocative.

6. *My sister refuses to face the fact that our mother can no longer manage living on her own and will need to make other arrangements. I work at an assisted living center, and my sister refuses even to come see the place. She is running herself ragged taking care of Mom, but insists that Mom remain in her own home. What should I do?*

It is not uncommon for conflicts among siblings to arise when eldercare decisions must be made, but these sisters could not even begin to have a discussion. In fact, although they were standing side-by-side when this question was asked, each ignored the other as she presented her own case. Fortunately, there was no immediate urgency, since their mother's needs were being met, and the caregiving sister, although struggling, was able to manage. Nevertheless, as they spoke with us it was apparent that trouble was in the making and would erupt in the not-too-distant future.

Our Understanding: We suspected that the actively caregiving sister was "hooked" on being the good sibling (see page 236). By taking on the entire task, she had effectively squeezed her sister out. The fact that her eldercare-experienced sister was making reasonable suggestions strengthened our conviction that longstanding sibling rivalries were at the root of the problematic behavior. Because of this, and since there was no immediate need to make a change, we suggested that our questioner wait until an opportunity arose—such as a worsening of the mother's condition or inability of her sister to continue giving adequate care—to intervene. At that point, suggesting a visit to the facility would probably make more sense, and a meeting with an impartial professional might be arranged. We reassured her that by monitoring the situation and by staying abreast of appropriate resources to use when the time came, she was still part of the caregiving team.

7. *My mother, who lives far from me, is having memory lapses and will soon be unable to continue living independently. I need her to sign an application to get her on the waiting list of an assisted living facility near my home, but she keeps forgetting to do so. I'm tempted to forge her signature, but that doesn't seem like the right thing to do.*

This caring son was caught between being respectful and being practical. Since his mother was not opposed to the move, the issue was one of proper procedures for the early stages of dementia, not one of coercion.

Our Understanding: Since there was no disagreement about the move, this situation, while distressing, was not serious. We supported the son's desire to ensure that his mother was involved in this major decision, and we recommended that he ask someone his mother trusted to sit with her while she signed the papers, and then to take charge of sending them to the son. His mother was aware of her memory lapses, so we suggested that gently confronting her on her repeatedly forgetting to sign the papers, and telling her about his proposed solution, would probably be the best way to handle the matter.

8. My parents, both 93 and suffering from dementia, live in Florida, in a senior community. Although their care, provided by private home health aides, has been satisfactory, there have been several recent crises for which I had to fly down to take care of things. I don't mind doing this, but lately, as soon as I come home, my father calls and complains that I never come to see them! I feel terrible having him think I am neglectful, and I know that things are only going to get worse. Should I try to move them closer to me? I've looked into options, but none of the facilities I checked out can promise to take care of them as their dementia progresses.

This long-distance caregiver was facing an increasingly common dilemma, as parents who retired and moved to Florida or other retirement areas become unable to manage on their own. Her first reaction was to move them back home, so she checked out local options. Wanting to make things as easy for her parents as possible, she tried to locate a facility that would be appropriate for both the early and later stages of dementia. Not able to do so, she was now reconsidering her decision to move them, but felt at a loss as to how to proceed.

Our Understanding: This woman's biggest struggle was with her own guilt at being thought an uncaring child. Her failure to convince her father that she had just visited was seriously interfering with her ability to make sound decisions. When we reviewed the specifics of her parents' care, we assured her that there was no need to take immediate action. We also reminded her that it was the *dementia*, not her father, that was accusing her of neglect, and that she was certainly fulfilling her obligation as a caring child. Once that was established, she recalled options that had been mentioned by professionals in Florida, and we suggested that she check them out and compare them to what was available closer to home. We also suggested that while she continued to explore options she hire someone—either a geriatric care manager or other trusted person—to oversee her parents' care and keep her informed.

9. *My 95-year-old mother still lives on her own. Whenever I visit, she insists on preparing a big meal for me. The problem is that her cooking has deteriorated and I just can't eat it anymore. I still want to visit and don't want to hurt her feelings, but short of not visiting—or pretending to be ill—I don't know how to avoid her dreadful meals.*

This son had already cut down on his visits but was not happy with this solution. His mother had always been proud of her ability to cook and entertain lavishly, and needed to maintain the illusion that she could still do so.

Our Understanding: When a parent cannot be confronted on an issue, it may be possible to work around the difficulty to preserve the parent's pride. We reassured the son that even compassion has limits, and that being a good child does not mean sacrificing one's health. We suggested several ways he could limit what was served while keeping the illusion alive that his mother was entertaining him. For example, since breakfast usually involves little or no cooking, he could schedule breakfast visits. Or he could drop in, unannounced, for a cup of tea or coffee. If necessary, he could even ask his mother to prepare only specific dishes for him (those she cooks acceptably), since they are his "favorites." The specifics of handling situations like this will vary, of course, but the principle is always the same: respect the need underlying the problematic behavior, and find an acceptable way to gratify it.

10. *My brother keeps pressuring me to put our mother in a nursing home. My mother is frail but still manages nicely with the help of*

a home health aide. She also does not want to leave her home of forty years. How can I honor my mother's request and still keep peace in the family?

As we mentioned before, sibling conflict is common as parents age. It usually reflects longstanding problems having nothing to do with eldercare. The woman in this dilemma was caught in the middle, between her mother and her brother, and she did not know how to extricate herself.

Our Understanding: Since the mother's current living arrangements seemed satisfactory, and were also what she clearly preferred, we wondered why the brother felt the need for change. Often the suggestion that a parent be institutionalized occurs out of anxiety and a desire to be done with the decision, even if premature. It also tends to be proposed when there is little awareness of what life in a nursing home is really like. We suggested that since the brother was the one advocating for change, he be encouraged to visit several nursing homes for himself and come up with some concrete suggestions for facilities that might be appropriate. We thought that the very act of checking things out might help alleviate the brother's need to do "something." At the completion of his investigation, the two siblings could compare his findings with the mother's current arrangements and determine, along with their mother, which solution made the most sense, both emotionally and financially. By proceeding in this manner, no one is put in the middle, alliances are avoided—that is, all options are placed on the table for discussion—and sounder decisions are more likely to occur.

11. My wife and I remarried in our fifties. We each have two grown children from previous marriages. What can we do to reduce the likelihood of conflict if end-of-life decisions must be made on our behalf?

This couple, having heard horror stories from other blended families, was trying to prevent the same from happening to them.

Our Understanding: When parents are clear about their needs and wishes, life is simpler for their children. This is especially true in the case of blended families, where alliances and conflicts are more likely to occur. To begin with, parents must complete living wills and health care proxies. They must be sure that the person designated to make decisions—hopefully someone with the support of everyone in the blended family—has a copy. This way there is no ambiguity about the parents' wishes. Burial preferences should also be clearly stated; any arrangements that can be made in advance should be taken care of. Children should be told of these preferences and the location of relevant documents. Any disagreement or conflict should be discussed openly and resolved as fully as possible. If a child understands the reasons underlying a parent's choices, he or she will be less likely to contest them later.

In a similar vein, parents should be sure that their wills are properly updated, to prevent confusion about the distribution of property after their deaths. Although legal documents can be challenged, this is less likely to occur when a child believes the documents reflect the parent's true wishes.

12. My family has never accepted the fact that I'm a lesbian. I would like my partner to make medical decisions for me if I am unable to do so, but I'm afraid that my family will try to take over. What should I do?

This question was asked of us privately, after an eldercare presentation. The woman was young, with no current health issues, but she recognized a devastating illness or accident can happen to anyone. She wisely decided to take action, but she was uncertain of the steps to take.

Our Understanding: This woman's concern was a valid one. In most states, the law automatically grants the right to make medical decisions to biological relatives, regardless of how long a gay or lesbian couple have been together. Even though this situation may change in the future, the time frame is uncertain, and rights still may vary from state to state. For this reason, individuals in committed gay or lesbian relationships should be sure that the documents outlining their wishes are properly completed. These documents include a living will, a health care proxy, hospital visitation authorizations, and a power of attorney. Parents and other family members should be informed of the person's wishes. The following Web site provides additional information: http://lesbianlife.about.com/cs/families/a/medicalrights_2.htm.

13. *My parents are in their seventies. My mother has dementia and is beginning to have trouble managing her daily activities. My father is fine, physically and mentally. Although they love their home, they're considering moving to an assisted living facility because of my mother's illness. My brother thinks this is a good idea, but I'm not so sure.*

This question is one of many we have been asked about assisted living. (There have been so many that we are devoting the entire next chapter to this subject.) The woman was correct in doubting that a single facility could adequately meet the very different needs of both parents. She also knew that her father had misgivings about his ability to care for his wife at home, though he was willing to give it a try. However, her brother was pushing for assisted living because he wanted to spare his father the burden of caring for his wife.

Our Understanding: We feel strongly that when one parent is willing and able to care for the other, it is wise to support that decision. Home care is a realistic option for someone in the earlier stages of dementia. The father could obtain the practical help and emotional support he needed through the local branch of the Alzheimer's Association. There he could get information to help him cope with her current level of dementia, and guidance for the future. In addition, he and his daughter could join support groups, if desired, to lessen feelings of isolation, to increase knowledge, and to learn practical tips from others in their situation. And when the mother's dementia worsened to the point that home care was no longer realistic, placement in a nursing home would make sense to everyone. If the home were nearby, the father could visit and still maintain a life for himself.

We feel strongly that when both parents move into an assisted living facility together but only one of them needs institutional care, they are taking a risk. It is not realistic to expect an institution to provide both dementia care and activities appropriate for a fully intact senior. Although the needs of the ailing spouse are primary, those of the well-spouse must also be considered. We know of well-spouses who moved into institutions with their partners, then left on their own, feeling guilty at having "abandoned" a loved one. We know of others who remained but deteriorated because the environment was so depressing and under-stimulating. When two parents have very different needs, it's extremely important to find a solution satisfactory for both.

14. *You say that when it comes to eldercare decisions, it's important to keep everyone "in the loop," but I don't agree. Why should I include my brother in planning for our parents' care? He hardly ever talks to them. He won't lift a finger to help out, and he constantly criticizes everything I do. Do I really have to complicate my life?*

To the man who raised this question, involving his brother made no sense at all. Why, he wondered, would we want to make his caregiving responsibilities more arduous than they were already?

Our Understanding: We're convinced that taking the easy way out—in this case keeping the toxic brother "out of the loop"—creates worse problems later on. We certainly don't advocate making a caregiver's task more difficult than it needs to be. But in cases like this there is more to be lost than gained in excluding the problematic family member. When serious decisions need to be made, such as putting a parent on life support, any conflict among family members may be reason enough for a physician or a hospital to disregard the parent's wishes. At critical moments, siblings and others whose opinions carry legal weight may appear out of nowhere and try to impose their own wishes. Some doctors will disregard a parent's advance directive, even if properly executed, when there is dissension among family members about the course of action to be followed.

Keeping everyone informed of the parent's wishes and of the contents of advance directives and other end-of-life documents is no guarantee that things will run smoothly. However, even if siblings or other relatives disagree with a parent's choices, they may respect those choices if they are certain that they truly reflect the parent's wishes.

15. My mother is severely demented and in a nursing home. I visit occasionally, but she cannot talk and appears not to know who I am or why I am there. I have two teenage sons, both of whom remember their grandmother as a warm, vital woman. Neither wants to visit her now, preferring to remember her as she was. I respect their choice and have allowed them not to visit. However, my two sisters think I am wrong, and that in permitting my sons not to visit I am failing not only my mother but my sons as well.

The woman who brought this up had her own misgivings about the value of visiting someone in the last stages of dementia. She wanted to be a good daughter, but she wondered how much her trips to the nursing home really mattered to her mother. Given the distressing nature of these visits, she saw no point in forcing her sons to see their grandmother in her current condition, and she felt her sisters had no right to tell her what to do.

Our Understanding: We strongly supported the woman's decision to honor her children's wishes. Visiting a loved one in the late stages of dementia is difficult even when done willingly. Forcing such a visit on her children because it is the "right thing to do" seemed pointless at best, and potentially traumatic. More important, regardless of the correctness of her decision, this woman had the right to run her life and raise her children as she saw fit. Since she was not shirking her own obligation to her mother, we encouraged her to stand up to her sisters and do what seemed right for her family.

16. *My father has Parkinson's disease, but he can still get around without much trouble. My parents love their home and have many friends in their neighborhood. They want to stay where they are for as long as they can, but their home may not be suitable for them much longer. What can we do to help?*

The dilemma this man was facing is not unusual. Although the disease in question was Parkinson's, the issues are pertinent to any progressive, debilitating illness, such as ALS or MS. He explained that his parents lived in a two-story home and that negotiating the stairs would eventually become a problem for his father. He had gone with his parents to a seminar about Parkinson's, and they learned that other changes were recommended, such as replacing round faucets and doorknobs with levers. Before doing anything, he wanted to be sure that he included everything possible to allow his father to remain safely in his own home.

Our Understanding: We were touched by this man's caring and desire to do the right thing. We were also aware that his good intentions needed to be supplemented by hard information about the needs of people with Parkinson's. We saw his job as having many parts: gathering information about what would be needed and what was available, obtaining an in-home assessment of his father's needs, and deciding, with his parents, which changes to make. We referred him to the American Parkinson's Disease Association (see Resources), where he could obtain literature and find out about programs in his area. We also suggested he contact the American Occupational Therapy Association for help in locating an occupational therapist who could do an in-home evaluation and suggest the appropriate adaptations.

17. *I just came back from visiting my parents for the holidays. I was shocked at how much their health has deteriorated since I last saw*

them. They now seem to be too frail to be living alone. What should I do?

This woman was in a state of shock and panic. On her last visit, her parents had seemed fine. During the year they had told her about doctors' visits for various ailments, but they had not indicated any significant difficulties or changes in their routine. Their daughter was shaken by what she perceived as great deterioration. She felt guilty and neglectful. She also felt an urgency to do something about it.

Our Understanding: While we think it is likely that this woman's parents were not functioning as well as they did a year ago, we doubt that the situation was as urgent as she saw it. We know that barring serious illness or accident, most people adapt to age-related losses of functioning. They may not move as quickly as they once did, but they can still get around. Certain tasks, such as cooking, may take longer to complete but can still be performed. When a parent's level of functioning is accepted on its own terms, and not in comparison with what it once was, it is seen in a different light.

We suggested to this woman that she speak with her parents and share her reservations about their ability to remain in their own home. In response to her concern, her parents might be willing to allow a professional assessment of their situation and explore options. If they felt no need for change, however, and there was no immediate risk to health or safety, we advised the woman to back off for the present, but to keep closer tabs on her parents, either by visiting more frequently or by having someone else look in on them from time to time.

So there you have it: the questions and comments we've heard most often since *Are Your Parents Driving You Crazy?* was first published. We hope you can apply the suggestions they contain to your own eldercare situation, and let them guide you to a course of action that is respectful, reasonable, and realistic.

CHAPTER EIGHT

The Assisted Living Option

Points to Ponder

Of all the questions we have been asked since the publication of the first edition, by far the most frequent have to do with assisted living facilities. These questions are most often raised by adult children, because most newspaper ads and other marketing efforts for these facilities target them, not their parents. Presented attractively, these facilities appear to be an ideal choice for an elderly parent. And for some parents, they may be. However, in other instances they are not as wise a choice as other, less costly, options. When they are selected too hastily, the results can be far from ideal.

It's possible to determine the feasibility of the assisted living option by asking certain critical questions. Once it has been determined that assisted living would be appropriate, you can proceed to evaluate the soundness of the particular facility you and your parents are considering.

Is the Assisted Living Option Right for My Parents?

The following questions can guide you in making a decision about whether assisted living is a realistic option for your parents.

1. Have my parents indicated in any way that they are no longer comfortable living at home?

Most parents want to "age in place," in their own home and neighborhood. They almost certainly have routines that make their lives pleasant and predictable, such as watching television in the evening, sitting in a favorite chair, and eating ice cream. Being uprooted needlessly is cruel, even when well-intended, and can result in depression and physical deterioration. Assisted living professionals have cautioned us that increasingly, parents enter assisted living because their children want them to, not because of any felt need on their part. Once there, they may be frightened and upset by the lower level of cognitive and physical functioning of other residents. Because of the high cost of assisted living, many residents are entering at a later point in their decline, when they are already physically or cognitively compromised. The condition of these residents may be traumatizing to your parents.

2. My parents are having a hard time staying in their own home. Does this mean that they have to move?

A parent may have fallen, or may no longer be able to cook or shop. Sometimes when parents have been ill or hospitalized, they are no longer able to resume living at the same level as previously. However, even when there is objective need for some kind of change, a move may not be the best option.

Aside from cost, there are some important advantages to keeping a parent at home. Parents who are comfortably mobile in their own house or apartment, where they know every bump and crack, may be unable to negotiate long corridors to a dining hall without a wheelchair or walker. Communal dining halls come with a greater noise level and increased demands for socialization, and this combination may drive a hard-of-hearing parent into isolation. If one of your parents is still healthy enough for independent living at home, moving both of them—as often happens—can be devastating for the well-spouse. And whether a resident is well or not well, loss of favorite foods or routines can lead to a litany of complaints.

As an alternative to a move, a parent's home can often be made safer in many ways. For instance, remove area rugs, improve lighting, and rearrange furniture. If medical equipment is needed, such as a hospital bed, rent it. If steps are a problem, have a chairlift installed or make a downstairs den into a bedroom. Bathrooms can be made safer by the installation of grab bars. Pivoting door latches, which are easy to grasp and rotate, can replace doorknobs. Monitoring services are available; some rely on electrical devices located in pendants and bracelets to summon help, others rely on motion detectors to confirm that a parent is engaging in usual activity. If even more help is needed, there are agencies that provide in-home care. The Visiting Nurse Service, for example, can provide ongoing, professional care. Food or prepared meals can be delivered. Adult day care and respite care can provide relief for a well-spouse or an exhausted child.

Often these changes are sufficient to allow a parent to stay at home. Though the costs for these changes and services can add up, they are often less than moving to an institutional setting.

We have found that too many adult children are unaware of the wide range of products and services that are readily available. If a parent wishes to remain at home, it may be practical and feasible to honor that request.

3. If it's clear that my parents can no longer live at home, is an assisted living facility the right choice?

Many assisted living facilities are inappropriate for parents who need a great deal of care. Most are structured so that each additional service involves added cost. If your parents are likely to need a great deal of help at present or in the near future, or if they are too ill to take advantage of the activities included in the fee, an assisted living facility may not be a wise choice.

Always find out the criteria for discharge from an assisted living facility. Inability to pay is one, but other factors also operate. For example, even though some facilities have dementia units, they may not be equipped to provide the high level of care needed in the later stages.

For parents not yet needing nursing home care, but whose condition is expected to worsen, a facility that offers a continuum from assisted living to true end-of-life care may be the appropriate choice. For parents who have extensive medical issues, a nursing home may be the best choice.

4. *Do I know the actual costs involved, including extra charges for the services my parents need?*

Most facilities provide fee schedules for services that go beyond the norm. But "beyond the norm" can mean different things. There may be charges for such things as personal products and laundry service. When arriving at a true figure for the cost of care, be sure to make a realistic assessment of the items and services needed by your parents. Assisted living facilities also vary in how you pay. Some require a lump sum up front, others just monthly payments. As you would before committing to any contract, be certain you understand the terms of the agreement you are making with the facility.

In determining what you can afford, consider not only your parents' financial situation but also any additional money you or your siblings would be required to contribute. You would not want your parents to have to move because money has run out.

If the move would require that your parents sell their home, is this something they are prepared to do? Do you know current market values? Do you know the cost of any repairs that will be needed before sale? Although some children feel obligated to do whatever is necessary to provide for their parents' comfort regardless of cost, it should be possible to find solutions that are both acceptable and affordable.

5. *What is the physical layout of the facility? What is the ethnic and socioeconomic makeup of the resident population?*

Often, as parents give up driving, and as their friends die or move away, they are left relatively isolated. One reason for considering an assisted living facility is to combat that isolation. However, if a parent is infirm and the physical layout difficult to negotiate, your parent may find getting around—a prerequisite to socializing—a daunting task. More specifically, can your parents climb stairs? Can they manage a self-service elevator?

In addition, if your parents are not with *their* kind of people (that is, those with similar backgrounds, values, etc.) they may find it difficult to make friends. For some parents, a smaller, more intimate facility that caters to particular populations may be a more practical and comfortable choice than a larger, more "mainstream" and luxurious one.

6. *Are my parents joiners? Are the activities provided likely to be of interest to them?*

If your parents enjoy staying in large hotels and going on cruises, if they adore large dining rooms, an upscale assisted living facility may be a perfect solution. However, if they enjoy privacy and find chatting with strangers tedious, institutional living may be akin to purgatory. Your aim is to make their quality of life better, not worse. In that vein, take a careful look at the lifestyle that characterizes the institution and the activities provided to see whether these are things your parents would truly enjoy. Your aim is to find a place that matches their temperament, style, and interests, as well as meets their physical needs.

7. *Would my parents have to give up activities that matter a great deal to them, like cooking or going to church?*

It is both unrealistic and cruel to ask your parents to give up activities or practices that really matter to them. If your mother loves to cook, but the apartment unit she will be living in only contains a tiny microwave, she will miss doing something important to her. Perhaps there is a kitchen she can use? If your father is an avid woodworker, is a shop available? If not, can accommodations be made? Think of your parents' day-to-day routine. Compare it to what is offered, and consider what would be gained or lost by the move. Be sure that the place you select will meet *your parents'* needs.

8. Is the food consistent with what my parents like to eat? Have I sampled the meals there?

No facilities acknowledge serving "gray soup," but we've eaten some pretty awful meals at some pretty fancy places. If food matters to your parents, be sure the quality and variety are acceptable. Given the number of meals your parents will eat over the course of their stay, this seemingly trivial consideration can become a major source of unhappiness.

9. Am I able/willing to oversee the care my parents will receive?

Your caregiving does not end once a parent enters an assisted living facility (or nursing home, for that matter). Regular visits are mandatory—not just to remain connected with your parents, but to be sure they are receiving the care they are entitled to. Any complaints your parents have need to be investigated. For this reason, it makes sense to select a facility that you, a relative, or a friend can visit regularly without undue inconvenience.

How do I Evaluate a Particular Assisted Living Facility?

Let's suppose you and your parents have decided that assisted living makes sense and is feasible financially. It's time to begin visiting a number of facilities. What do you look for?

While there are many considerations to be made in evaluating an assisted living facility (see Appendix A), the first is, "Is the facility I am considering licensed and accredited?" Before considering any facility seriously, you must determine whether it meets criteria established by state and private agencies.

As of this writing, there is no federal licensing of assisted living facilities. Licensing requirements vary widely from state to state. Until relatively recently, in most states, assisted living facilities were licensed only as residences. As such, they were required to meet few criteria, none of which had much bearing on the care of elderly people. Over the past few years, a consumer-oriented movement has gotten underway requiring that these facilities meet licensure criteria appropriate to the health care organizations that they are. As a result, many states have imposed more stringent licensing laws. In addition, these laws are constantly being changed in the direction of stricter, more realistic, requirements.

To find out what the licensing requirements are in your state, call your Office for the Aging (the listing will be in the blue pages of your telephone directory), or conduct an Internet search. One excellent Web site, www.CareScout.com, maintains an online database that provides up-to-date information on each state's licensing requirements.

Accreditation by the Joint Commission on Accreditation of Healthcare Organizations (JCAHO) is a sign that an institution is striving for excellence above and beyond state mandates. For years, the Joint Commission has been the national leader in accrediting healthcare organizations. Ask the administrator of any facility you are considering whether it is JCAHO-accredited. (The less stringent your state's licensing requirements the more important it is to find out whether the facility you are considering meets JCAHO-standards.) You can find out more about JCAHO and its accreditation criteria at its Web site, www.jcaho.org.

In addition to making sure that the facility you are considering is licensed and accredited, we recommend strongly that you carry out a more detailed, multi-dimensional evaluation. The Assisted Living Checklist located in Appendix A provides excellent and comprehensive guidelines. As a minimum, we urge you to do the following:

- Visit the facility you are considering several times at various points in the day. Observe activities. Speak with residents and family members. Eat the main meal.

- If a support group is available, attend at least one meeting to get a sense of the ongoing issues at the facility.

- Find out how staff members and other employees are selected, and what kind of training they are given. Ask what the staff-to-resident ratio is, during both daytime and nighttime. Find out what kind of nursing care is provided, including the credentials of nurses and the hours of coverage. Ask whether a social worker is on staff and what his or her function is. Then speak with the social worker if possible.

Regardless of which facility you choose, you, your parents, and anyone else involved in the decision need to agree on the following:

- Who will be the central contact for the facility? Who will be designated as the health care proxy? It is simpler if the same person serves both roles.

- What are the family's wishes regarding resuscitation, intubation, and hospitalization? These should be communicated clearly to the facility prior to admission. An up-to-date living will should be provided as well. The time to make tough decisions is before an emergency arises.

The recommendations contained in this chapter come from two sources: the experiences, both good and bad, of people with whom we have spoken, and the advice of assisted living professionals who have worked with families for many years. We hope you will take them seriously. We're confident that if you do, you and your parents will be spared needless distress.

❧

CHAPTER NINE

In a Nutshell

Guidelines for a Caring Partnership

Here are the essential points we've made throughout this book. They can serve as a review, a source of inspiration, or as an aid to regaining perspective. They will help you form a caring partnership with your parents.

Take Care, Don't Take Over. Your primary job is to help your parents retain as much independence as they can for as long as possible. Never confuse *taking care* with *taking over.*

Propose, Don't Impose. Show respect. While you might know what's best for your parents, you might also be wrong. To be safe, offer your thoughts as suggestions, not as orders.

Talk <u>with</u> your parents, not <u>at</u> them. Involve your parents in every decision that affects them. Be guided by the principle "nothing about me without me."

Empathize, don't infantilize. Try to put yourself in your parents' shoes to keep from patronizing them. Remember to focus on *ability*, not *disability:* a healthy respect for your parents' abilities, regardless of their chronological age, is essential to avoiding conflict. In your planning, keep in mind what they *can* do, not just what they *can't* do.

Timing is everything. The right help at the wrong time will be rejected. The wrong help at the right time will be useless. Success lies in offering the right kind of help at the right time.

Offer just enough help and no more. Doing too little is uncaring; too much is insulting and may create dependencies. To determine the right amount of help, ask your parents about their needs. Know what you're trying to achieve. Be prepared to monitor the results of the help you provide.

Sometimes good enough is good enough. Most elderly parents are resilient, creative, and realistic. Their living arrangements need not be perfect for them to be happy, safe, and satisfied.

Plan ahead. It's never too early to plan for the future. As any long-distance cyclist will tell you, drink before you're thirsty, eat before you're hungry, rest before you're tired. For example, prepare a living will *before* a health crisis arises.

Prepare yourself. Your most important preparation is internal. Know what to expect and what issues are likely to arise. Anticipate your *own* emotional reactions as well as those of your parents. As parents age, you will be entering their lives in a different way. Expect to feel dismay, distress, sadness, and frustration. These feelings are part of caring. Adjusting to this new twist in your relationship is a major task for you and them.

A problem is not a crisis. Assess the urgency of a situation before doing anything. No matter what situation you face, stay C-A-L-M:

> C—*communicate respect:* don't preach, judge, shame, or blame.
>
> A—*ask permission before you act:* you'll accomplish more doing things *with* your parents than doing *for* them.
>
> L—*listen more than you talk:* understand what your parents' needs and concerns are.
>
> M—*maintain emotional perspective:* don't get "hooked"; don't satisfy your own needs at your parents' expense.

Assisted Living Checklist

༄

The following checklist is reprinted by permission of www.CarePathways.com. We find it to be unusually comprehensive. Should you wish to locate others, we recommend that you conduct an Internet search using a question such as "What should I look for in an assisted living facility?"

First Impression
- Do you like the facility's location and outward appearance?
- Is the facility convenient for frequent visits by family and friends?
- Is the facility near a shopping and entertainment complex?
- Can the resident access a medical complex easily?
- Is public transportation available/accessible?
- Are you welcomed with a warm greeting from the staff?
- Does the staff address residents by their names and interact with them during your tour?
- Do you notice the residents socializing with each other and do they appear content?
- Can you talk with residents about how they like living there and about the staff?
- Is the staff appropriately dressed, friendly and outgoing?
- Do the staff members treat each other in a professional manner?
- Are visits with the residents encouraged and welcome at any time?
- What percentage of the apartments has been rented and is occupied?
- Is there a waiting list? If so, how long do they estimate it will take to be admitted?

Living Area and Accommodations
- Is the floor plan well designed and easy to follow?
- Are doorways, hallways, and rooms accommodating to wheelchairs and walkers?
- Are elevators available for those unable to use stairways and handrails to aid in walking?
- Are floors of a non-skid material and carpets conducive for safe walking?

- Does the residence have good lighting, sprinklers, and clearly marked exits?
- Is the residence clean, free of odors, and appropriately heated/cooled?
- What is the facility's means of security if a resident wanders?
- Are the common areas in general attractive, comfortable, and clean?
- Is there an outside courtyard or patio for residents and visitors? Can they garden?
- Does the residence provide ample security and is there an emergency evacuation plan?
- Are there different sizes and types of units available with optional floor plans?
- Are single units available and/or double occupancy units for sharing with another person?
- Does the residence have furnished/unfurnished rooms? What is provided or what can residents bring?
- May residents decorate their own rooms? Is there adequate storage space?
- Is a 24-hour emergency response system accessible from the unit with its own lockable door?
- Are bathrooms private with handicapped accommodations for wheelchairs and walkers?
- Do all units have a telephone and cable TV, and how is billing handled?
- Does a kitchen unit have refrigerator/sink/cooking element and can food be kept in residents' units?
- May residents smoke in their units or are there designated public areas?

Moving In, Contracts, and Finances

- What's involved with the moving in/out process? How is the initial needs assessment done?
- Does the assessment process include the resident, family, facility staff, along with the physician?
- Is there a written plan for the care of each resident? Is there an ongoing process for assessing a resident's need for services, and how often are those needs evaluated?
- Is the facility affiliated with a hospital or with a nursing home?
- Will your room be held for you should you require a hospital/nursing home stay and are there charges for your room while you're away?
- Is there a written statement available of the resident rights and responsibilities?
- Is a contractual agreement available that clearly discloses health care, accommodations, personal care and supportive services, all fees, and

admission and discharge provisions?

- How much is the monthly fee? How often can it be increased and for what reasons? Is there a limit on the amount of increase per year? What is the history on monthly fee increases?
- What are the specific costs for various levels or categories of services?
- What additional services and staff are available if the resident's needs change?
- Is there a procedure to pay for additional services such as skilled nursing care and physical therapy when the services are needed on a temporary basis?
- When may a contract be terminated and what are the policies for refunds and transfers? Is there an appeals process for dissatisfied residents?
- What happens if funds are depleted and full payments can no longer be made?
- Is there any government, private, or corporate program available to help cover the costs?
- Find out what the payment schedule is and if residents own or rent their unit.
- Are residents required to purchase renters' insurance for personal property in their units?
- Do billing, payment, and credit policies seem fair and reasonable? May a resident handle his or her own finances with staff assistance if able? Must a family member or outside party be designated?

Health, Personal Care, and Services
- Can the facility provide a list of available services and are residents and families involved in developing the service agreement? Who provides these services and what are their qualifications?
- Is staff available to provide 24-hour assistance with activities of daily living (ADLs) if needed? ADLs include dressing, eating, mobility, hygiene, grooming (bathing, toileting, incontinence).
- Does the residence have programs for Alzheimer's, other dementias, and other specialized areas?
- Is staff available to assist residents who experience memory, orientation, or judgment losses?
- How are medical emergencies handled? Does the residence have a clearly stated procedure for responding to medical emergencies? Is there an arrangement with a nearby hospital?
- Does staff supervise/assist residents in taking medicine? May residents take their own medications?
- Does the residence's pharmacy provide delivery, consultation, and review of medicines?
- Does staff assist in making arrangements to have nursing and other

medical care? Does either a physician or a nurse make regular check-ups? Or to what extent is medical care available?

- Are physical, occupational, or speech therapy services available, and is there a staff person to coordinate home care visits from a nurse, physical therapist, occupational therapist, etc.?
- Are housekeeping, linen service, and personal laundry included in the fees, or are they available at an additional charge? Are onsite laundry facilities available and convenient?
- Does the residence provide transportation to doctors' offices, a hair-dresser, shopping, and other activities desired by residents, and can it be arranged on short notice?
- Are pharmacy, barber/beautician, and/or physical therapy services offered onsite?

Social and Recreational

- What kinds of group and individual recreational activities are offered and who schedules them?
- Is there an organized activities program with a posted daily schedule of events?
- Do volunteers and family members come into the residence to partic-ipate in or conduct programs?
- Does the facility schedule trips or go to other events off the premis-es?
- Do residents participate in activities outside of the residence in the neighboring community?
- Are the resident activity (social) areas appropriate and desirable to the prospective resident?
- Are there supplies for social activities and hobbies (games, cards, crafts, computers, gardening)?
- Are religious services held on the premises or arrangements made for nearby services?
- Are there fitness facilities as well as regularly scheduled exercise classes?
- Does the residence create a sense of community by allowing residents to participate in certain activities or perform simple chores for the group as a whole?
- Are residents' pets allowed in the residence? Does the facility itself have pets? Who cares for them?

Staff

- What are the residence's practices and philosophy regarding staffing?
- What are the hiring procedures and requirements for eligibility? Are criminal background checks, references, and certifications required?
- Is there a staff-training program in place and what does it entail?

- Is staff courteous to residents and to each other? Are requests for assistance responded to promptly?
- Is the administrator, or an appropriate staff person, generally available to answer questions or discuss problems, and would you be comfortable dealing with them on a daily basis?
- Does the facility have a volunteer program or is it affiliated with any student clinical programs?

Food

- Does the residence provide three nutritionally balanced meals a day, seven days a week, and how does the menu vary from meal to meal?
- What about special diets—does a qualified dietitian plan or approve menus? Is each resident's weight routinely monitored?
- Are residents involved in menu planning and may they request special foods?
- Are common dining areas available and when can residents eat meals in their units?
- Does the dining room environment encourage residents to relax, socialize, and enjoy their food?
- Are meals provided only at set times or is there some flexibility? Are snacks available?
- How many meals are included in the fee? If a resident becomes ill, is tray service available?
- Can residents have guests dine with them for an additional fee? Is there a private dining room for special events and occasions, if desired?

Licensure and Certification

- If the state requires the residence to be licensed or certified, does it have a current license/certification and is it displayed?
- If the state requires the administrator to be licensed or certified, does she or he have a current license/certification?
- Is the facility a member of a trade or professional association?
- What reputation does the facility have in the community? How long has it been in business? Is it in good financial health? Does the facility follow generally accepted accounting procedures?
- If the facility is sponsored by a nonprofit organization and managed under contract with a commercial firm, what are the conditions of that contract?
- Is there a resident council or organization through which residents or their family have a means of voicing their views on the management of the community?

Notes for My Own Situation*

Dilemma: _____

_____

Clarify the Problem

1. Does everyone agree a problem exists?

_____

_____

2. How urgent is the problem, really?

_____

_____

3. What is behind your parent's problematic behavior?

_____

_____

4. What's hooking you?

_____

_____

5. Who must be included in problem-solving discussions?

_____

_____

6. What is your goal?

_____

*For an electronic version, go to www.vandb.com/apdc_worksheet.html

Solve the Problem

1. List in the chart the needs your solution must satisfy.

2. List in the chart a few possible solutions.

3. Complete the chart, analyze the choices, select the best solution.

GOAL: _____

	POSSIBLE SOLUTIONS			
	Do nothing			
NEEDS				

4. Conduct a Murphy's Law analysis.

_____

_____

5. Decide how you will carry out your plan.

_____

_____

6. Evaluate your progress.

_____

_____

Resources

AARP
601 E Street NW
Washington, DC 20049
PHONE: (888) 687-2277
E-MAIL: member@aarp.org
WEB SITE: www.aarp.org

55 ALIVE/MATURE DRIVING PROGRAM:
WEB SITE: www.aarp.org/life/drive

AMERICAN AUTOMOBILE ASSOCIATION FOUNDATION FOR TRAFFIC SAFETY
607 14th Street NW, Suite 201
Washington, DC 20005
PHONE: (202) 638-5944
FAX: (202) 638-5943
WEB SITE: www.aaafts.org

THE AMERICAN OCCUPATIONAL THERAPY ASSOCIATION, INC.
4720 Montgomery Lane (or P.O. Box 31220)
Bethesda, MD 20824
PHONE: (301) 652-2682
WEB SITE: www.aota.org

AMERICAN PARKINSON DISEASE ASSOCIATION
1250 Hylan Blvd., Suite 48
Staten Island, NY 10305
PHONE: (888) 400-2732 or
(800) 223-2732
WEB SITE: www.apdaparkinson.org
E-MAIL: apda@apdaparkinson.org

BETTER HEARING INSTITUTE
515 King Street, Suite 420
Alexandria, VA 22314
PHONE: (703) 684-3391
FAX: (703) 684-6048
E-MAIL: mail@betterhearing.org
WEB SITE: www.betterhearing.org

COMFORT HOUSE
189-V Frelinghuysen Avenue
Newark, NJ 07114-1595
PHONE: (800) 359-7701
FAX: (973) 242-0131
E-MAIL: customerservice@comfort-house.com
WEB SITE: www.comforthouse.com

DRIVERS.COM
c/o PDE Publications, Inc.
310-5334 Yonge Street
Toronto, Ontario M2N 6M2, Canada
PHONE: (416) 767-4885
E-MAIL: pde@drivers.com
WEB SITE: www.Drivers.com

ELDERCARE LOCATOR
National Association of Area Agencies on Aging
PHONE: (800) 677-1116
WEB SITE: www.eldercare.gov

NATIONAL ACADEMY OF ELDER LAW ATTORNEYS
1604 North Country Club Road
Tucson, AZ 85716
PHONE: (520) 881-4005
FAX: (520) 325-7925
WEB SITE: www.naela.com

NATIONAL ASSOCIATION OF AREA AGENCIES ON AGING
1730 Rhode Island Ave., NW
Suite 1200
Washington, DC 20036
PHONE: (202) 872-0888
FAX: (202) 872-0057
WEB SITE: www.n4a.org

NATIONAL ASSOCIATION OF PROFESSIONAL GERIATRIC CARE MANAGERS
1604 North Country Club Road
Tucson, AZ 85716
PHONE: (520) 881-8008
FAX: (520) 325-7925
WEB SITE: www.caremanager.org

NATIONAL ASSOCIATION OF THE DEAF
814 Thayer Avenue
Silver Spring, MD 20910-4500
PHONE: (301) 587-1788
FAX: (301) 587-1791
E-MAIL: NADinfo@nad.org
WEB SITE: www.nad.org

RONCO SALES ORGANISATION
T.B. Davies (Cardiff) Ltd.
Penarth Rd.
Cardiff CF118TD
United Kingdom
PHONE (within UK): 029 2071 3000
WEB SITE: www.ronco.co.uk

SELF HELP FOR HARD OF HEARING PEOPLE
7910 Woodmont Avenue, Suite 1200
Bethesda, MD 20814
PHONE: (301) 657-2248
FAX: (301) 913-9413
WEB SITE: www.shhh.org

VISITING NURSE ASSOCIATIONS OF AMERICA
99 Summer St., Suite 1700
Boston, MA 02110
PHONE: (617) 737-3200
FAX: (617) 737-1144
E-MAIL: vnaa@vnaa.org
WEB SITE: www.vnaa.org

U.S. LIVING WILL REGISTRY
523 Westfield Avenue (or P.O. Box 2789)
Westfield, NJ 07091-2789
PHONE: (800) LIV-WILL or
(800) 548-9455
E-MAIL: admin@uslivingwillreg
istry.com
WEB SITE: www.uslivingwillreg
istry.com

Index

Sidebars, which contain resource information, are listed here in italics.